Darko, T
practice ~ live
Live it!
FM.

LIVE IT!

Your Courageously Authentic Life

Frank C. Maloney MBA, CPCC

Copyright © 2012 Frank C. Maloney and FCM Publications

All rights reserved. No part of this book may be reproduced by any mechanical, photographic, or electronic process, or in the form of phonographic recording; nor may it be stored in a retrieval system, transmitted, or otherwise copied for public or private use without the prior written permission of the author.

Library and Archives Canada Cataloguing in Publication

Maloney, Frank C., 1968-
    Live-it! : your courageously authentic life / Frank C. Maloney.

Includes bibliographical references.
Issued also in electronic and audiobook formats.
ISBN 978-0-9881485-0-5

    1. Self. 2. Self-esteem. 3. Self-acceptance. I. Title.
BF697.M34 2012   158.1   C2012-905370-8

FCM Publishing
65 High Park Avenue, Suite 2314
Toronto, Ontario
M6P 2R7

Note to reader: This book is not intended to dispense medical advice or prescribe the use of any technique as a form of treatment for physical, emotional or medical problems without the advice of a physician. The products and information contained in this book are not intended to diagnose, treat, cure or prevent any diseases or medical problems. The information is provided for educational purposes only. In the event you use any of the information in this book for yourself, which is your constitutional right, the author and publisher assume no responsibility for your actions.

Printed in Canada

Table Of Contents

<u>Acknowledgements</u>

This book is the culmination of many years of living and contemplating. I would like to thank my mom, my friends and family (you all know who you are). I'd also like to give a special shout out to PublishandPromote.ca and their dedicated associates who helped me tremendously in all facets of marketing and production getting this to be the book in your hands today.

At the beginning of each chapter there is a courageous real life story of authenticity. All of these stories have been included as they were written.

I want to deeply and warmly thank all the wonderful people who had the courage to share their true stories about learning to live an authentic life, no matter the cost or outcome. Their stories confirm and reinforce the thesis of this book: everyone can step into their truth, grow and thrive.

Live It! is a very small (but meaningful) snapshot of the lives of these fantastic people, whom I am blessed to have attracted into my life, and who live authentically like me. I know all of them personally and can tell you that their stories confirm the strength of their authentic characters. I hope you have so many good people in your life.

"Be yourself, everyone else is taken."

~ Oscar Wilde

Prologue

Introduction to Courageous Authenticity

"The strongest force in the universe is a human being living consistently with his identity." [1]

~ Tony Robbins

---

1   http://www.quotegarden.com/be-self.html

Introduction to Courageous Authenticity

Welcome to Live It! My name is Frank Maloney, MBA, CPCC and I am a teacher, certified coach, mentor, human experience inventor and experimenter, author and Law of Attraction specialist. This work contains what I believe to be the essence of what it takes to live a powerful and meaningful life: authenticity. The meaning I am assigning to authenticity is that of *"being real", "being your true self", "living your truth",* etc. Authenticity is purity. I have discovered authenticity on my journey through personal growth, learning to first recognize, then accept, then appreciate, like and ultimately love myself, flaws and imperfections included. The "love myself" part is a work in progress to be honest and authentic!

After two very traumatic life-altering events five years ago and again three years ago (covered in Chapter 2) I embraced 100% authenticity and integrity as my salvation. Over the last year, after a third incredibly challenging life event, I have reframed my authenticity as my own personal secret weapon or trump card. In my humble opinion, authenticity is messy, it is often inconvenient, confronting, and can be brutal to ourselves and others. However, like water it is inherently cleansing, freeing, nourishing, sustaining and elemental to living a great life. The same way roiling rapids or large ocean waves can throw you around, a calm placid lake can comfort and refresh and a pond can caress your very soul. Authenticity is purity and like water has a magnetic effect on all those around us especially in a world in which many people live inauthentically.

Quitters never win and Winners never quit.

I don't think people consciously try to live inauthentically.

Live It: Your Courageously Authentic Life

I think inauthenticity is a product of a modern society and culture that has many of its values mixed up and/or missing; a culture that espouses and deifies promiscuity, material possessions, achievement at any price, easy and short term solutions, and shying away from taking personal responsibility.

"Our secular society isn't working, and in fact it is self-destructive. Perhaps the real evil is the spirit of this society - its self-interest, money, runaway desire, or ambition." [1]

We live in a world where we wear masks and often feel we are somehow not "enough" or too "flawed" as we mistakenly assume we are unlovable because of our flaws. What we don't realize is that our imperfections and quirkiness make us human and give us a chance to connect and relate to each other one on one. When you are trying to be something/someone you are not, you essentially lose the essence of what makes you unique and desirable. Realize that the masks you wear to appear better come from ego and lack (scarcity perspective of the universe vs. abundance to which I dedicate Chapter 2). The masks cover fear of judgment leading to fear of rejection and loss. The fear stems from childhood when parental abandonment could literally kill us and that vibration is very negative and unattractive (physically and literally as it doesn't attract good things; like attracts like).

I feel that life is about being your authentic self, or more specifically, your Most Brilliant Self (as opposed to your other inner voice, your Saboteur Trickster Most Pathetic Self, STUMPS).

"Your purpose in life may be to become more who you are and more engaged with the people and the life around you, to really live your life." [2]

---

1 Moore, Thomas, *Dark Nights of the Soul*, page 67

2 Moore, Thomas, *Dark Nights of the Soul*, page XIV

Being our real and authentic selves, flaws, warts and all is far from what so many people are experiencing. Authenticity allows us to automatically, either really like or dislike each other. If you're wearing a mask, you don't know how people really feel about you. The fact that many may dislike your true self is a good thing as those people will naturally go away, making room for those who truly and deeply like you. In this work I aim to allow you to embrace your authentic self: warts, imperfections, flaws and all. Let's put away the masks and save them for costume parties and Halloween!

> **Authenticity is a muscle! No matter where you are right now, you can move towards more authenticity.**

If someone likes your authentic self, there is no fear of losing them as they like who you really are from the start. As a result, powerful, nourishing and lasting relationships based on true common perspectives and interests can form. Trying to be everything to everyone (brainy, sexy, sporty, successful, artistic, etc.) doesn't work in target marketing for cars nor does it for people. Being authentic allows your target market (the opposite sex) to really see you as a unique and attractive proposition with multiple facets and quirks.

Being happy with yourself and who you are attracts others who are real as well. People who are okay with also being flawed make much better friends. Being flawed is being human and the world needs more humanity. Being interesting and different is attractive, and someone who has many passions and interests is incredibly attractive. Passions and interests should be things that feed our soul, not TV and mass popular culture which is a negative vibration (worry, fear and scarcity (lack) perspective).

3

Authenticity Muscle

Authenticity is a muscle! No matter where you are right now, you can work towards living with more authenticity. If you are not used to being transparently honest, a.k.a. your true real self, it will at first feel scary, difficult and too unachievable. Realize that's the exact same way most people look at going to the gym and working out. The 23% or so of North Americans who work out regularly worked through that. They persevered, became committed and live healthier and more sustainable lives.

Every single one of them felt afraid, uncomfortable and daunted at first. They didn't just say, *"Well, I'll never be fit, I quit!"* Quitters never win and winners never quit!

Authenticity is like a muscle in that the more you use it, the better it works. Most people live their lives with sporadic flashes of authenticity but soon crawl back behind their "safe" persona/mask. Make no bones about it, striving to live fully authentically all the time is a very difficult path. As with all things worthwhile in life, those who persist succeed. That's why so many don't stick to it, and end up leading weak lives that aren't really theirs! Or at least not their "Most Brilliant Self" life!

--

Typical Client Challenges

As a breakthrough mentor, coach and inspirational Law of Attraction speaker, I've discovered that a very primary client/participant complaint centers around controlling (or lack of controlling) one's life or the enjoyment of feeling in control; steering it as it were. You might even experience some of these statements daily:

"My life's out of control."

"I'm so overwhelmed!"

"I'm not doing what I REALLY want to do, and I'm depressed about it."

"I can't ever seem to make everyone happy and even if I do then I'm miserable!"

"I can't make a decision."

"I need to hire you to get my life back on course/track!"

"I don't know what to do, I'm stuck/at a crossroads!"

"When will my life get easier?"

"I'm numb all the time."

"Our relationship just doesn't work anymore."

"I feel I'm just going through the motions, not really living, just existing."

These are all symptoms of a deeper problem. The problem according to me:

We are very powerfully trained from birth to ignore our natural tendencies to take care of ourselves first and we unconsciously learn to live inauthentic lives.

We are conditioned (our parents meant well but they learned from their parents) to think that prioritizing our own needs and wants ABOVE all others' needs is SELFISH (painted as very bad in general). All the religions of the world espouse some version of *"You must sacrifice YOURSELF FOR OTHERS to be good!"* dogma. Most people are selfish in non-productive ways. Selfishness has been equated with everything from being "evil" and "bad" as a kid, to not being a team player as an adult or in a company.

Live It: Your Courageously Authentic Life

If you don't take care of yourself first you are empty and have nothing to give anyone else!

Shame (guilt) is a powerful negative emotion (with its two brothers, insecurity and unworthiness - #21 on the emotional scale (ES)[4] just slightly above the worst feeling emotions at #22: Fear, Despair, Depression, Grief, Powerlessness. These are just below #20: Jealousy. (We will cover the emotional scale later).

> **We carry deep-seated anxieties around, wanting to be liked by everyone, even if the truth is, WE don't like everyone.**

Think of aircraft emergency instructions: "If the aircraft cabin is losing pressure you are to put your own oxygen mask on first, then help others including your own children."

Another example is to think of your life as a container. This container holds all of your wisdom, thoughts, ideas, soul, life experience and emotions. People who have tried, failed and retried have HUGE co[1]ntainers and can handle anything and everything life throws at them (more joyfully and easily too!).

#1 Regret Of The Dying

The number one regret of dying people is that they didn't live authentically!

---

1   *Please refer to the Emotional Scale in Appendix 2: The Abraham Hicks Emotional Scale*

Nurse Reveals the Top 5 Regrets People Make On Their Deathbed [1]
By Bronnie Ware (who worked for years nursing the dying)

"I wish I'd had the courage to live a life true to myself, not the life others expected of me. This was the most common regret of all. When people realize that their life is almost over and look back clearly on it, it is easy to see how many dreams have gone unfulfilled. Most people have not honored even a half of their dreams and had to die knowing that it was due to choices they had made, or not made. It is very important to try and honor at least some of your dreams along the way. From the moment that you lose your health, it is too late. Health brings a freedom very few realize, until they no longer have it."

--

Live It! Activity #1: Ask yourself this question: Will I regret not trying/ doing this? If yes, always DO IT! As Tony Robbins says, *"If I can't, then I must!"*

List the 5 things you must do NOW or you will regret:

1. _____

2. _____

3. _____

4. _____

5. _____

--

---

1   [i] http://www.inspirationalchai.com/Regrets-of-the-Dying.html

One reason we don't act authentically is that we are fearful of judgment, not only from others but also from ourselves. We were told by numerous people, in various places at many times that we weren't (at some or all levels) good enough. So the ego (often as a small child) adapted and created what it thought was a "better" persona; a persona that would attract less anger or disapproval at a young age was a very "smart" adaptive process with which to protect us.

Unfortunately we grow up but don't realize that the danger is gone and we still pretend to be something we are not. Your mind says, *"You are not enough, don't be your true self, you will be judged, laughed at and not liked, you are not good enough and don't want to be abandoned"*. The media most people consume support this insecurity with its focus on perfect models, successful people and keeping up with the Jones'. All this in an ill-fated attempt at consuming the latest "lifestyle-improving" products/services. We carry deep-seated anxieties around wanting to be liked by everyone, <u>even if the truth is we ourselves don't like everyone.</u>

--

Live It! Activity #2: What character flaws from youth have you adapted for survival/coping in order to develop a "better" persona (a.k.a. a mask)? List three.

_____

_____

_____

--

Major Life Shifts

People who are overwhelmed by their life and problems are in that state because they didn't carefully grow in life and challenge (stretch) themselves enough in many different ways. In my own personal and professional experience, people create new life pathways in one of two ways.

Major life shifts come in two varieties:

1. "External to us" events (family death, illness, separation, job loss) or...

2. "Internal to us" events (career burnout, depression, etc.)

When a certain "tsunami" of a life event capsizes our weak, untested "boat", we suffer tremendously.

Sometimes we self-create the tsunami because we can't bear to live in the inauthentic way we are living. We feel empty and unfulfilled. The things, ideas, events and people that used to excite us no longer do. Beyond that point (everyone's timeline is different) our life changes. It becomes more painful to "NOT CHANGE" than to "CHANGE". As Tony Robbins[1] puts it, you need leverage on yourself and you need to get DISTURBED (not annoyed, inconvenienced, sad, angry, etc.) but well and DISTURBED ENOUGH! Then AND ONLY then, will you have all the leverage you need.

I'm An Elephant!

As an example, one of my clients was severely obese. In the past she said to herself and others, *"I'm a little overweight, or I have/need to lose a few pounds."* It is obvious that she was trying to minimize her pain. It only prolonged the unwanted torturous situation; she was lying to herself and others and didn't believe it!

---

1   Tony Robbins, www.tonyrobbins.com

To really get disturbed she (with my assistance) became courageously authentic and said something like, *"I'm an elephant! I'm really %$#@ huge! I need a circus tent to cover my ___!"* Many people, maybe even you just recoiled in horror at her last sentence. This is good! It confirms my point that you and I have been trained to be politically correct and inauthentic! I can bet you that the person who believes the second sentence (butt as huge as an elephant's, etc.) has enough pain/leverage to change now. Often humans are only motivated by tremendous pain. This is unfortunate because growing on your own terms allows you to handle bigger and bigger pains (as our "experience container" grows).

> *It's too bad that too often the wrapper in movies "masks" the message that being your true self is the greatest liberation and freedom a human can experience.*

--

Live It! Activity #3: In what area of your personal life are you MOST deeply unsatisfied with? Score each of them on a level of current satisfaction out of 10 (where 1 is horrible and 10 is fantastic).

Friends	/10	Family	/10
Fun & Recreation	/10	Health	/10
Money	/10	Personal Growth & Spirituality	/10
Significant Other/romance	/10	Career	/10
Physical Environment	/10		

Will you become more authentic? Where do you choose right now to be more authentic? Are you okay with how others may/

will react? If not, you must really feel the cost of being inauthentic. What does inauthenticity rob you of and why?

Hollywood Courage

No one said courageous authenticity was easy. Courage and honesty are hard at first, but like any habit can be honed. If it wasn't hard more people would be authentic. Authenticity is not something that gets a lot of media play in general. Although if you look at what any Hollywood movie plotline tantalizes constantly, it is **authenticity**. Almost every "coming of age" storyline has in it someone trying too hard to be "normal" or "acceptable" only to be strongly rejected. By the end of every movie, the real, authentic person gets the girl/boy, dream job and/or whatever they always wanted.

It's too bad that too often the wrapper of the movie "masks" the message that being your true self is the greatest liberation and freedom a human can experience. I will use the term "masks" often in this book as it is a great metaphor for the discussion on authenticity (and I have a fascination with masks too!).

> *Courageous authenticity: you are ALWAYS striving to be your true self, you follow and act in accordance <u>to your heart and your true wants, needs, feeling and desires!</u>*

Abraham Hicks Emotional Scale

The Abraham Hicks Emotional Scale (see Appendix 2) is incredible and a must-study for you. I will use it extensively in Live It! It works by enabling you to seek thoughts that feel better and with each new thought you can climb the scale and continue to experience better and better feelings. Firstly, you climb the scale by thinking less toxic emotions (for example, if you are in Hopelessness (#22 on the ES) and you get Angry (#17 on the ES), anger feels a lot better than hopelessness.

At first you climb slowly, but now after years of practice I can jump from #22 to #1 within hours! It's very powerful! Additionally, as you rise towards #8 (Boredom, the only neutral emotion) your vibration increases. Positive thoughts produce positive vibration which attracts many other similar thoughts, events, ideas and people so that better gets better and worse gets worse. Once you've passed Boredom it starts feeling really good the rest of the way. At the top of the scale, the best feeling emotions are: #1 Appreciation, Joy, Freedom, Empowerment and Love and they're what everybody wants but few regularly achieve. I am also quite partial to #2, Passion, as I now live my life with serious and frighteningly strong, unbridled and fully expressed passion of myriad types!

--

Growing Our Life Container

People who don't grow due to laziness or lack of desire, have stunted, small (child-like) containers and their containers are often upside down due to living in Worry (#17 on the ES) and Fear (#22 on the ES). Even when life's abundance is pouring, it doesn't fill them because they are too immersed/drowning in their problem as a result of focusing on negative thoughts that are coming from too far down the emotional scale. When we are going through a bad period and good things happen we sometimes say, "Yeah but it's not going to last." And of course it doesn't as we are not even appreciating what is there (Appreciation is at the top of the ES at #1).

"What you focus on grows, what you resist persists and what you ignore haunts you no more!" [1]

---

1   Maloney, Frank, Cobra in the Closet, page 205

Our Taking Doesn't Deprive Others

A word on abundance... Many people are afraid to take everything life can give because they believe it will DEPRIVE others of something (and they are good people who don't want to abuse others). I used to feel this way before I understood the Law of Attraction. You don't have to look very far to realize the universe is ridiculously, immensely abundant and all limitation is a creation of our minds and media. Look at a field of flowers, unlimited; look at the ocean, abundant; look at the cosmos, billions of stars.

The universe is comprised of vibrational energy. The higher you vibrate (emotions #7 to #1 on the ES) the more you are attracting people, events and circumstances at that same level! Like attracts like! Similarly, the universe abhors a vacuum, so the more you ask (by feeling good, appreciating and loving) the more the universe will supply. I have the following on my vision wall (we will cover vision boards in chapter 7): "**Supply follows Demand.**" The universe is incredibly abundant; any thoughts that come from lack or limitation are lies from your STUMPS. I discuss abundance further in Chapter 3.

--

Courageous Authenticity Defined

Let's take a look at Live It!'s subtitle, "Courageous Authenticity." There were many definitions but this is my favorite and how I mean to express the word:

Courageous [1] : *"The quality of mind or spirit that enables a person to face difficulty, danger, pain, etc., without fear; bravery."* I disagree with the "without fear" part. Courage means feeling the fear and doing it anyway because you know it's authentic and needs to be done!

---

1   www.dictionary.com

Live It: Your Courageously Authentic Life

Authentic [1] (authenticity is the noun): *"Not false or copied; genuine; real."*

So if we put them together we get what I meant: **Courageously Genuine.**

Courageous Authenticity in YOUR life: Means you are thoughtfully and consistently striving to be your true self ALWAYS. You follow your heart and your true wants, needs, feelings and desires in spite of the external and internal pressure to be something else!

Once you are courageously authentic, so many of your daily challenges are no longer there as you are yourself no matter what. This authenticity is WHO YOU ARE BEING, NOT WHAT YOU ARE DOING. Therefore all thoughts and actions come from that place. It is the most powerful way to live as it is the real you. People will flock to you once you begin believing and living like this.

--

Others Will Be Threatened

A warning... many people won't like it! It's very confronting for those around you and especially for those closest to you. All their own inauthentic behaviors are tested, questioned and they may feel exposed. In order to maintain their congruence between their actions and self-image, most people will reframe your authenticity in a few different ways.

1. They may determine you are crazy.

2. They may think you are rude, full of yourself and without manners.

---
1 www.dictionary.com

3. They may think that YOU are inauthentic and are playing a game or wanting attention.

4. Any other thought that rejects you (is critical) out of fear or misunderstanding.

All of the above evaluations are easier to make sense of than the truth, which may be that they don't have the courage to be real so they keep their "safe" masks on, and judge those who do.

--

Claiming Your Abundance

Don't let the title Live It! mislead you into believing I am advocating claiming anything from anyone in a forceful, coercive and/or violent way, far from it. I am absolutely and always talking about taking/claiming the abundance you have created for yourself and that you deserve. This means abundance in relationships, joy, opportunities, income, growth, etc. Nothing more nothing less, fair is fair! The universe is always fair; it gives and receives in equal measure. If you give more (via helping and contributing to others without expecting return), the universe will give you so much more back, including joy, love, connection, appreciation, and freedom.

These are only ALL the things everyone is striving for, whether they know it or not. Being a fervent Law of Attraction practitioner and coach, I strongly believe the universe is an immeasurably abundant place (look at all the flowers or stars!). Also, look at the fact that the human mind is still unlimited in its abilities, light years beyond any computer.   A truly magical and perfect self-repairing, self-managing and self-regulating supercomputer! Additionally, the fact that every single human being is completely different from any (and all) others is utterly mind boggling!

> *We are taught from a young age, to think of others first, to play fair, to be "nice" and not be our true selves as it may hurt other people.*

Like Attracts Like

Not only is there MORE than enough to go around (ignore all media and negative people's "the world is scarce/fearful" thoughts), but the more you grab from the universe, the more it will CREATE abundance for others and YOU.

If for example, Steve Jobs hadn't formed a new vision for how people interact with their world, he wouldn't have created a better world for the rest of us to enjoy via electronic interfaces that felt natural. Had Steve been a "reasonable" and inauthentic "normal" (what does that even mean anymore?) person, we would not have benefitted. But he was authentic, and although many people hated working for him, they respected him and followed him because he was true to his authentic self to the very end.

This is a central and key concept to get your head around. Like attracts like; quantity and quality is reflected exactly back to you. If you don't like the life you created by all your choices and thoughts, you can change it. The thoughts you had one year, six months, three months, one month, two days, two hours, or two minutes ago led to the choices/decisions that led to the actions that created exactly where you are right now.

--

Getting Into Authentic Choice In Your Life

This book's purpose (among others) is to help to inspire you to make joyful, empowered and clear authentic choices for your life. It's also to help support you in ripping off your comfortable and safe (inauthentic) mask in order to reveal your most authentic self in all its splendid uniqueness and glory. Once that happens, you feel and ARE in control of your life. You then can choose without (or much less) guilt (#21 on the ES). You stop trying to please others (an impossible task really) and get ALL of your own life back. You will feel much lighter and freer as you can be yourself.

--

It's Not Working

Being assertive, self-centered and certain are <u>not</u> qualities deeply respected (sometimes not even tolerated) in our modern society. More often, Empowerment (#1 on the ES) or Passion (#2 on the ES) is confused with the cockiness borne from overcompensating for Insecurity/Unworthiness (#21 on the ES). This happens because few people actually DO live consistently in authenticity, and most are new and unsure of its feeling and vibration. They are very different because the power from #1 emotions (Empowerment, Love, Freedom, Joy and Appreciation) is really strong and certain.

We are taught from a young age to think of others first, to play fair, to be nice (whatever that means!). As adults, how is that working out in general for society at large? It DOESN'T work. Divorce rates, drugs, alcoholism, child abuse, pornogrified and cheapened sexuality and intimacy support this point. Often, it seems that the values of today's lifestyle center around fame, power, money, promiscuity and "ease" of living at any cost. I use "ease" to signify that our quest to simplify and make life convenient loses great learning. Then we wonder why life seems to lose much quality and depth.

--

Our Thoughts Create Our Experiences

We create (attract) with our thoughts, emotions and feelings all the people, events and experiences we receive in our lives (what we label "good" and "bad"). Even these labels are faulty as "bad" events often expand our container (all that we can handle). Most of my clients tend to learn more from difficulty and failure than from success.

Whatever you are TAKING is there to TAKE based on your thoughts, vibration, actions and energy. Those who are NOT putting huge amounts into life (we "put" into life with our authentic selves giving our all) also don't get much back. Then they blame outside forces and circumstances, refusing to take responsibility. Those who seem blessed by all manner of abundance coming to them have created this abundance with their predominant thoughts, actions and vibrations. Once we get clear on loving ourselves and feel we deserve more, the universe obliges by giving us more and we can TAKE MORE! You can't take what you haven't created for yourself.

--

What You Should Never Take

One last point before jumping into the topic... I believe it is important for me to distinguish which things we SHOULD take as opposed to what we SHOULD NEVER take and why.

1. Your time in this life. Time is short and really the only thing that is limited in life, thus its inestimable value. It is limited for everyone

2. and is the only thing we all have that is the same for everyone. We all have seven days a week and twenty-four hours in a day.

   Procrastination is the thief of time and very sneaky.

3. Your life too seriously. Life is fun and light when you decide to live that way. If you choose difficulty, it will be difficult because the universe can't buck your vibration. Seriousness is usually a byproduct of fear and rigid thinking and living. Look at someone like Richard Branson; he's like a kid having a great time. It's easy, not hard!

4. What doesn't belong to you or is offered to you. This can apply from stealing to taking other's time without their consent. If you must take anything by force, know that the rage vibration is very toxic (Rage, #20 on the ES). A word here on Power vs. Force. Force is the main means portrayed/modeled in media (and the world) to get things done. It is typically aggressive, coercive and sneaky. Contrast Force with Power. Power is from within. It is earned by the person's vibration and who they are being. Think Gandhi defeating the British military without any bloodshed. It is said that one person in alignment (with their source energy, living in the higher emotions) is more powerful than thousands out of alignment.

5. Decisions/choices that do not feel right to you. If you don't feel good about it, don't do it! Your compass of emotions is your best guide for knowing if you are on or off your path, nothing else.

> *No matter how much you respect or love another person, their advice is just that, advice.*

6. Your life and its grandeur and potential for granted. You are absolutely unique in every way, act like it.

7. <u>Your "knowing how life works" story, seriously.</u> The minute you think you have life figured out, you cannot be any further away from wisdom. Once you really believe you don't know ANYTHING, that's when wisdom has arrived. You are then open to all and can enjoy learning again, putting ego aside.

8. <u>Other people's advice as gospel.</u> No matter how much you respect or love another person, <u>their advice is just that, advice.</u> It is usually based on their perspective of life, their experiences, worries and fears, which are completely different than yours. It's okay to use portions or aspects of people's advice in making your opinion. Globally, all opinions should be considered suspect as the agenda of the person giving it is often unknown, unspoken and fear-based.

--

What You Should Always Take

1. <u>All opportunities put in front of you that resonate with you (connect to your soul and heart).</u> You always learn more from the opportunities you take (even and especially if you fail, remember, we learn more from failure) than by not taking a chance. By not trying you miss all the learning that occurs when taking chances. Fortune favors the courageous and brave. Not making a choice IS A CHOICE, a choice devoid of any courage or learning. NOT making a choice is always the worst option as others then make their own choices, benefitting themselves. If you don't make a choice you lose the insight and self-actualizing facets of trusting yourself. Taking charge and making choices leads to feeling in charge of your life.

Live It! Activity #4: Time for **YOU** to make some choices! What are you saying "YES" to? Identify and clarify what you are saying "NO" to. Once you know one (Yes or No) then the opposite is clearer.

Example: "*I am saying YES to running 3miles every day. I am saying NO to watching TV or pushing the "snooze" button an extra three times. Another example, "I say YES to working part time and being frugal and say NO to working full time for more money and additional stress.*"

To say "Yes" to _____I must say "No" to _____

To say "Yes" to _____I must say "No" to _____

To say "Yes" to _____I must say "No" to _____

To say "Yes" to _____I must say "No" to _____

To say "Yes" to _____I must say "No" to _____

--

2. Life as a great game of exploration and adventure! Doesn't that sound like a great way to see it, instead of a great series of problems, hurdles and disappointments?

Your #1 quest in life should be,
"WHAT do I want and WHY do I want it?"

---

3. You always need to get clear on WHAT you want and WHY you want it. Once you know what you want, life becomes so much simpler as you can choose powerfully and quickly and not look back with guilt. This is your #1 quest in life, "*What do I want and why?*" Once this is clear, a multitude of "difficult" or even seemingly "impossible" situations can be dealt with from a

place of empowerment and certainty. That's an amazing way to live!

4. <u>The present moment as a gift.</u> Another name for a Christmas or birthday present is gift. That is what the present moment is; a once in a lifetime gift never to be experienced again. All of our power of decision and choice must necessarily occur in the present moment (since we can't time travel yet).

A dream without a plan or action is simply a fantasy.

The word decision is derived from Latish and means, "*To cut off all other options.*" Much of your daily practice should center around being present to all the beauty of nature and the wonderful people and world around you. Get out of your head and into your heart! Any time we worry or are apprehensive (Fear), we are DEFINITELY NOT PRESENT! In the present moment is where all action can occur. Most people spend much too little time in the present moment. We go back to the past and feel guilt or anger, or we think of the future, which is good if we see it as positive.

Many people simply dream of a better future. A dream <u>without a plan</u> and action is simply a fantasy.

--

Live It! Activity #5: Name four activities you could begin immediately in order to be more present. Examples, yoga, breathing, exercise, walking, etc.

_____   _____

_____   _____

Useful Tips On Choices

Spend as much time gathering information on decisions/ choices. If you can't make a choice or do something about the decision, then put it aside and enjoy the present. Many of our best choices come when we are present doing something else.

Let's jump right into how you will LIVE IT! Live your life and experience all the abundance already waiting for you! Better yet: LIVE the life you've always wanted but probably didn't think you ever deserved.

> *Many people lose their sense of fun and trade it in for a sense of "maturity" once they become adults. What a shame!*

At the beginning of each chapter I have included a real life personal story of courageous authenticity to confirm and prove that real people do follow their authentic path and to inspire you to do the same.

--

A Courageously Authentic Life: Segment By Segment

At this juncture some examples of authenticity in different areas of life may be helpful to orient you. Please refer to Appendix 1, The Wheel of Life. The Wheel of Life[1] is simply a visual representation of most of our life areas. I use it to find out my clients' level of satisfaction with each of their life areas. As an example, one client may have put Money at number 3 or 4. This has an impact on all his/her other life areas, from sharing time and events with others (significant other, family and friends), to what they can do for fun and recreation, their health (if stressed about money), their physi-

---

[1] *Kimsey-House, Co-Active Coaching, pages 222-224*

cal environment, and even what types of personal growth they can afford. So all the areas are interrelated like a matrix.

--

Live It! Activity #6: Fill in the Wheel of Life in Appendix 1. Then look at each area and how it impacts your other life areas. For example, if you scored low in *"Health"*, what's the impact on your spouse (*Significant Other* on the wheel)? What about your *"Family and Friends"*, your ability to have *"Fun and Recreation"*, your *"Career"*? Do it for all areas. How comfortable is the ride of your life?

--

Authenticity In All Of Our Life Areas

I've listed out all the sections for clarity here.

Friends and Family: In this life area, authenticity could be speaking your truth and being honest even at the risk of annoying or hurting others. It might mean reducing or cutting exposure to those who habitually hurt you or are too negative or simply don't add to your life. Especially with family, our obligations to "do the right thing", "it's your own blood", "blood is thicker than water" often mask the fact the relationships are severely dysfunctional and are destroying us (and the other parties). Being authentic means being honest and let the chips fall where they may. For some, authenticity may mean cutting family members off. For others, it's being real with themselves and realizing that's who they are, quirks and all. As long as you are okay with it, it's your life!

--

In relationships, think of authenticity as a brush fire clearing out the weak relationships and making room for new growth.

<u>Significant Other:</u> Take a similar approach here. Speaking your truth and asking for what you need ensures your mate is always working with the same information you have. Having the courage to be authentic with your partner will open up an infinite amount of complicity and connection. If you are walking around being inauthentic and your partner is too, who knows what the actual state of your relationship is? You don't have anything solid or real on which to build a connection that truly thrives sustainably (a lifestyle that sustains us is replenish and energizing).

Most inauthenticity stems from the fear that our partner will not like us if they really know us; that they will not accept us for our flaws and/or worse, reject and leave us due to our imperfections. An authentic couple realizes that if their true(Most Brilliant) self is not acceptable to the other party, it is time to move on anyway as the relationship is a lie/farce.

The fearful (Fear, #22 on the ES) person wants to hang on to their partner as long as possible as they feel incomplete and not enough (#21 on the ES, Insecurity, Unworthiness) alone. In summary, authenticity strengthens most couples AND will terminate an unsuitable relationship quickly, clearing the way for a better one based on truth. A useful metaphor is to think of authenticity as a brush fire clearing out the weak relationships and making room for new growth.

> *If you are always tired, you can't enjoy all life has to offer.*
> *Energy is the currency of life.*

Authenticity may mean coming clean on some bad things you did to your partner. It could also mean CHOOSING to carry the guilt as it was a unique, one-time transgression and has been dealt with (to not hurt the other partner). This will create a new chapter together, or end the relationship, but both are better than lies and living in fear of the "what-ifs" in a relationship that is a lie.

--

Fun & Recreation: This is where we get to let the little boy/girl inside us out to play and have fun. Too many people lose their sense of fun and trade it in for maturity once they become adults. Soon the person is boring and bored because they try to be serious or mature. What a shame! What makes young children and pets amazing to us is their unbridled fun and adventurousness while getting into trouble. I say, who cares if people say you are going through a midlife crisis, etc? Where in your life could you be more authentic in having fun and doing crazy things? For me, my motorcycle riding, beach volleyball, video gaming and love of mixed martial arts keep me smiling. Most people could use more variety and excitement in this area of their life experience.

--

Health: Here, being real means an honest evaluation of where you are and taking your health seriously. You cannot lie to yourself that it's just a few pounds or dress/pant sizes. Your body is the most perfect creation ever and should be treated as the only vessel for all of who you are. We are only given one body, treat it with respect! Without vibrant energy (not big muscles) you can't be as authentic in other areas of your life. If you are always tired, you can't enjoy all life has to offer. Energy is the currency of life and opens us to all the possibilities of being human.

--

<u>Money:</u> Being authentic here is about enjoying your money but not racking up huge debts. Debts are an extension of spending more than you have, and are very inauthentic! Living within/below your means allows much more authenticity. It also removes stress and increases freedom, both of which are boons to authenticity. It's hard to be real when your reality (your OUTSIDE world) is an empty bank account and your bills are piling up. However, your current situation was created by your past decisions, thoughts and vibrations. There is always a lag time between thinking new thoughts and taking new actions and your stuff (all that you want) arriving! You can and should make new decisions today so you can improve your future.

--

<u>Personal Growth:</u> Being authentic here, means not lying to yourself. What are you consistently doing to grow as a person? Remember, in nature a plant is thriving or dying, and we are the same. Examples of personal growth include but are not limited to:

- Any spiritual, prayer, meditation or contemplation practice.

- Reading books, listening to or attending personal growth seminars/workshops and hiring a coach.

- Taking any type of class on a topic you are interested in or simply curious about.

- Challenging your mind in new and diverse ways helps you to grow and staves off most age-related mental degeneration. The brain creates new neural pathways to deal with new information and situations.

- Travel helps you to grow as you are taken out of your comfort zone.

> *Our careers should at the very least allow us to be our authentic selves. At best our careers can help us become MORE authentic than we were before.*

Physical Environment: Here being real is about where you live and your appreciation of it. Does your environment at home nurture and recharge you? Do you sleep well there? Is the noise reasonable? Of all the Wheel of Life segments, this one is the easiest to impact immediately. Spruce it up, make it homey or simply move. At work, the same process applies.

--

Career: This one is very important as many people chase money and not their passions (I also made that mistake a few times with negative results). Chasing success and money divorces us from what our heart tells us and is a sure recipe for misery. What we do in our life for work and sustenance also has to nourish our soul, challenge us and help us grow as a person.

We spend more time at work than literally anywhere else except maybe our beds, and that's a long time to NOT be excited about what we are doing. Being authentic doesn't necessarily always mean quitting your job, though it might. It may mean realizing you don't get a lot of passion from work and being okay with that, but ensuring you DO get HUGE passion outside of work. In my belief however, this is a short term solution as eventually we need to start being who we truly are in our careers as well. Additionally, if you don't love your work, you won't push yourself to be better there.

I believe one of our greatest roles in our lives is our careers/ vocations. A career can also mean being a stay-at-home mom or dad, which is definitely a very important career for so many. Our careers should at the very least allow us to be our authentic selves. At best, our careers can help us become <u>MORE</u> authentic than we were before and push us to grow as a person. When you wake up and feel thrilled about what you do you can truly say, *"I'll never work another day in my life!"* with pride. What a way to live!

--

"They say that people change over time when the truth is, they just become more of who they really are." [1]

---
1 http:www.coolquotes.com/categories.php

Chapter 1

My "Live It" Experience

"It is better to be hated for what you are than to be loved for something you are not."

~ Andre Gide

My "Live It" Experience

Courageous Authenticity Real Life Story: **Persistence Pays Off**

"I wanted this particular job in Toronto, longing with and desperation – even just at 22 years of age and living in my parents' basement – to leave the small town of barely 3,000 people that I grew up in. I thought to myself: "If I don't get this job, I'll never leave here." I did not get an interview despite my good qualifications and enthusiasm – lots of it – and decided to drive my beat up Honda to this particular Corporation's head office to look into the matter myself. No one had returned my phone calls for an explanation (this, too, was before the "internet age"). I waited and waited in the lobby – two whole 8 hour days in fact – for someone to meet with me. Nothing. Nobody. I just grew more persistent. Reception asked me to leave. No. A manager asked me to leave. No. "We will call security." "Call them." They came and asked me to leave. No. They carried me away. I cried. I drove back home. By the time I got home the next day my answering machine was blinking. There was a message from the Corporation: "Sir, there's been a terrible misunderstanding and we would like to grant you an interview." I got back in my Honda and drove back the very next day. The following week I was working in that very place. And the most amazing part of that entire story? My phone cord was not connected to the jack in the wall. I should not have got that message. But you know what? They sure got mine. And that's what really mattered."

~ Sean H.

--

My (Rocky) Path To Authenticity

I will recount my story not to profess it is THE way or the only or right way to Live It. It is simply a good place to start in the journey to courageous authenticity. Additionally, it is my experience. Perhaps this will uncover clues for you as to how to go about becoming your own version of fully authentic. Once you become authentic, you can never go back. Like a butterfly can't become a caterpillar, nor should it want to! Authenticity is the Holy Grail. Authenticity is truly (and the term is completely over used and much too weak for what I mean) what I will call a life transforming process. I know, as I've been living it.

Surprisingly, transforming maybe too weak of a word for what I will describe. I am seriously and honestly trying to explain an almost CELLULAR change from what I was a few years ago. The same way you would look at a caterpillar next to a butterfly and be hard-pressed to identify them as the same species let alone the same animal, species and individual. Actually, the same DNA! It's that BIG.

Without going into gritty details, (like most)
I had some issues in childhood.

--

I think that a little history about me will add context and help you to become more familiar with me. I became a Certified Life Coach in 2008 at the age of thirty-nine after my life had basically hit a (third) rut that was significant enough to have me on stress leave from my teaching vocation at a local business college. My life prior to that had consisted of a relatively unsettled and painful path. As with most people, I had some issues in childhood.

33

My father left my mother and the country before I was born, and at the age of six a new stepfather made a ten year appearance. He was a completely selfish workaholic, unstable (maybe bipolar), often cruel, verbally and sometimes physically abusive person. Mercifully, they separated when I was sixteen.

Throughout my twenties I was always unsatisfied and bored with most of the careers I chose and I changed jobs with the frequency most people change their socks. It was very unsatisfying and frustrating to never find a position that actually challenged me on multiple levels. Additionally, because I was a people pleaser it seemed that my life was very different from others and I was frightened and discouraged.

> *My (difficult) interpersonal relationships mirrored my job situation (as they often do) as we are whole individuals and all our life areas are interrelated and impact each other.*

Difficult Relationships

My interpersonal relationships mirrored my job situation. Life areas ALWAYS impact each other as we are whole individuals and all our life areas are interrelated and impact each other. [1] I often dated a woman (who was often wonderful) for a three to six month period before either leaving her or her leaving me.

About nine years ago I finally discovered a career that allowed me to be myself and to keep challenging myself. I began teaching Business at a local college, and in particular, Marketing. I had finally found a career that embraced my voracious learning and reading appetite. It additionally allowed me to be on stage and get paid for it which I loved and still do today as I speak regularly to audiences on Law of Attraction and authentic and inspirational living.

---

[1]   *See Appendix 1 Wheel of Life*

Soon, even teaching didn't satisfy enough and I became depressed again with what I felt were too few options. I had lost confidence in myself and my passions and abilities. I had three major depressive episodes from my late twenties to late thirties. The last one hit six years ago and I have been relatively stable since.

One thing that did change at that time for the better was a program I completed called Landmark Education[1] which allowed me to make one very powerful distinction: that lying was not the type of person I REALLY was and that a quality life was a life of integrity. After the program, I took their suggestion of calling up all the people I had hurt or lied to, to apologize and clean things up.

At that point a friend introduced me to life coaching and I found a language, context and tools that could help me deal with what pharmaceuticals had previously only masked.

> *I was fortunate (and competent and educated) enough to receive training from the world class inspirational speaker's company, Tony Robbins.*

I enthusiastically became certified (five courses, six months and one hundred hours of coaching to be certified) within one year and began building a small coaching practice part time as I continued to learn and master coaching. By late 2008, I was a certified coach and was looking for my next opportunity. I was fortunate (and competent and educated) enough to receive training from the world class inspirational speaker's company, Tony Robbins. At that time I was amazed at the new tools and incredible people that were going to be with me on the journey.

One such magical individual, I will call Dan, was my roommate and we bonded as long lost brothers would. I left Orlando without the job of coach for the company as I was deemed

1 www.landmarkededucation.com

"too entrepreneurial" or more of a "lone wolf" and not enough "by the book". I was devastated but not broken and made a promise to Dan to be in Los Angeles within a year. For the past six years, I've endeavored to never lie, and if I misspeak, I correct my error as soon as possible. So I knew I would be in L.A. very soon.

This lifestyle of integrity (minimal/no lies or deception) has quite a few advantages that I've discovered over these years.

a) It simplified my life.

b) It felt much better.

c) It allowed my subconscious to believe whatever I said implicitly and to help me.

d) It developed courage (as the consequences of telling lies are what hinder most people).

e) It increased my overall ability to handle whatever life threw at me.

--

Relocating To California

As I returned home I began creating a plan to relocate permanently to the Los Angeles area within seven months. My steady girlfriend at the time and her two daughters, seven and fourteen would join us on our odyssey. I took an unpaid sabbatical at the college. As my coach helped me to realize, if it didn't work out, I could always simply return to my life as it was with an amazing experience under my belt.

> *Within three days of relocating, life played another of its (sometimes) senseless and cruel tricks on our mere mortal plans and dreams.*

Within three days of relocating to Los Angeles, tragedy struck. My beloved girlfriend of 3 years, Aida had a brain aneurysm and was mere days from passing away. We made arrangements to have her daughters flown back (their dad flew to L.A. and left with them back to Toronto and I have not seen them since). The Red Cross helped us to arrange for organ donations. Sign whatever you need to in order to allow your organs to save another's life. I still have the beautiful Red Cross letter outlining how ten people's lives were saved with her eyes, lungs, kidneys, liver, pancreas and heart.

World Crusher

To refer to such a cataclysmic loss as devastating doesn't even remotely begin to define the soul-destroying, hope-crushing shock of losing your love and life partner so suddenly. I was shaken, pulverized to my very core and felt that a massive part of me had died with her.

I can still recall hugging her twelve hours before death and how peaceful and beautiful she still was and how I expected her to wake up. The mind plays nasty tricks, especially when in shock. I tried to continue to make it in L.A but it wasn't in the cards. I was lost, adrift, all that I had loved before now barely registering as a remote like. In fact, I had to relearn who I was and what I liked and disliked. We had prepared for many possible contingencies and challenges but not that one. Aida didn't believe in focusing on fear and had no insurance. The hospital tab was over $165,000 but was fortunately handled by a California insurance company.

> **When we are pushed far beyond what we think are our capabilities, our "container", which is our ability to handle life, grows enormously.**

After months of grieving and a few failed small business attempts (dating service and coaching), I began to recognize some positive elements of the experience. Do not confuse this with any reduction in pain; it was more of an acceptance of the situation. After nine months in L.A. I had burned through all my resources and racked up over $100,000 in debt. I chose to return to Toronto and somehow find the courage to continue to teach at the college. I imagine that was the only tether I could grab in my shell-shocked version of post-traumatic stress disorder.

Life Events Grow Our Container

One really powerful derivative of my partner Aida's death was that I felt that if I could survive that I could handle anything life threw at me, and it's true. <u>When we are pushed far beyond what we think our capabilities are, our "container"(our ability to handle life), grows enormously.</u> Additionally, it really taught me how precious life is and that we don't know how long we have so every moment should be lived as if it were our last. Many people talk about this but to live this way is completely different; it should not even have the same name. I believe that before the tragedy I was living as full a life as I could, limited by my fears, worries and general embarrassment of truly being my wildest, most crazy self. A better explanation would be that I existed and now I live. I met someone last year who had a serious brain tumor a few years ago and her life has also similarly transformed. She left a staid job to become a clown and spends her life making others happy!

I slowly began to rebuild whatever I could. I rented an apartment and bought some Ikea furniture. Ikea is a love/hate thing, but their furniture is great. You see, it was at Ikea that a carpet had fallen on Aida's head the night before her aneurism (doctors found no trauma to the head and confirmed she was always at risk). Her ex-husband decided to sue Ikea for her death and embroiled me in visiting the store with biomechanical engineers. I still like the store though (now that's a good brand!). One incredible thing that gave me strength was that even though I was at Despair, #22 on Abraham Hicks's [1] brilliant indispensable Emotional Scale [2], see Appendix 2, I never fell into a deep depression as I had in the past. Grief feels horrible, but it feels different than depression does.

> *For a few months things were great. We shared immense passion and she was very easygoing, (or so I thought).*

A Cobra In Disguise

Upon my return to Canada, I met a woman, fell in lust (the best way I can describe it) with her, and she moved in with me very rapidly. I was at a very low point in my life and she was at a very high point in hers. She kindly helped me get set up and lent me money to restart my life.

After a few months she lost her job and went into a serious tailspin and depression. She lost the will to live as she had invested/ created all of her (minimal) self-worth around her job, even though she loathed it. After losing her job, she gained thirty pounds and frequently sat watching movies. This went on for six months until I decided I was done and that she really wasn't who I thought she was (she had also shunned my family and became a recluse within a few months).

I left her and she attempted suicide by slitting her wrists within two hours in my bathroom. She tried again a few days later, taking sleeping pills while driving in a raging late March 2011 blizzard. After trying to help her drive to a friend's two days later she was

1   *Abraham Hicks, www.abrahamhicks.com*
2   *From the book "Ask and It is Given", pg. 114*

in despair (#22 on the ES) again and only two options seemed available: a) suicide or b) mental institution (she had already visited the psych ward three times in a week). As I was driving with her in her car it was as if a bolt of lightning struck me and I realized I should, could and would change that! I was incredibly empowered (#1 on the ES); it felt like my own personal eureka moment!

It was as if those eighteen months of pain and distress had served to compress (like a spring) all my desires, wants and dreams. Abraham Hicks calls this "launching rockets of desire" or "filling our vortex." [1]

I realized in that moment at a really deep level that: In any AND every moment we can make a choice that will change our destiny!

A Coach Rises From The Ashes

So I did just that. I created a whole new future possibility/ option and it was incredibly empowering! I decided to offer to coach her and turn her life around ONLY if she listened to my every word and accepted my coaching. She was shocked, freaked out, but grateful and accepted. At first she played dumb and wanted too many details, but I became very certain and powerful and took control. She accepted and you can read all about the whole sordid affair in my second book, *"Cobra in the Closet: An Inspirational Roadmap to Self-Discovery"* [2] about improving our relationships no matter what happens.

---

1 *The vortex is described as our vibrational escrow, or a non-physical place where all we have desired is waiting for us. We begin to bring those things, ideas and experiences to reality by allowing the abundance to arrive. We allow it by saying as often as possible in the top seven levels of the Emotional Scale - the higher we are on the scale, the more we are in the vortex.*

2 *Maloney, Frank, MBA, CPCC, Cobra in the Closet, http://bookstore.iuniverse.com/Products/SKU-000503615/Cobra-in-the-Closet.aspx*

> *If you DON'T: a) get clear about what you want b) know WHY you want it and c) ask for it clearly and powerfully you have NO right to wonder why you don't get it!*

I know that that was a big beginning. After the loss of Aida eighteen months before, I had completely lost interest in coaching, teaching, everything really. So I had done as much as I could in my severely reduced state of mental focus. I knew that night something REALLY big shifted, but I had no idea about the transformation I had just begun. It was as if I transformed in that moment. Honestly, if I had known, I wouldn't have believed it. However, the fact the *"Cobra in the Closet"* book exists is a constant reminder.

A Third Option

Initially, I only saw two options for my ex-girlfriend/client: re-hospitalization and or suicide. However, I created a new option where I would work with her as a coach to help her. It felt wrong at the time but I was desperate to help. I began working with my reluctant client. Coaches should NEVER attempt to coach family or friends as it can never work due to the close relationships and conflicts of interest.

I coached her seriously as I would with any client and by natural extension began coaching myself too. I loved it. It felt great to reconnect with that love of helping others to connect to their authenticity and help themselves. I reconnected with the clarity that this was my life path, *"to help, coach, educate and entertain"*. I began acting, speaking (language shapes our experience) and living in accordance. I really began believing it, because to me it was true.

I became more clear about what I wanted and started applying the idea that if I DIDN'T a) get clear about WHAT I wanted b) know WHY I wanted it and c) asked for it clearly and powerfully, I had NO right to wonder why I wasn't getting it!

> *Aiming for a "smooth" life is impossible for the simple reason that life is filled with uncertainty, variety, and complexities.*

My Live It! Experience

In an effort to move into developing your tools to Live It!, I created Appendix 3 to outline the results of my living courageously and authentically for over the last eighteen months. I didn't do it out of pride but as an example of the power of my experience and to maybe give you a glimpse of what awaits you once you become courageously authentic and Live It!

Life is a learning experience and we have a responsibility to learn from our mistakes. Too many people try to make their life as smooth as possible to avoid pain. Life is rarely smooth and trying to make it so is to take the wrong approach. A better question to ask ourselves is:

"How do I get to a place where I can handle anything the ocean of life throws at me and remain at my best (being authentic) in that situation?"

All this learning grows our "life ship" container so we can handle any and all situations that arise in our lives.

The Smooth Life Myth

Most people's objective/goal in life is to have a smooth life, one in which there isn't much turbulence or massive swings up and down. What could be better than a smooth life, right? Having this approach to life is impossible for the simple reason that life is filled with uncertainty, variety and complexity. To use a metaphor, life is like the ocean. An ocean is powerful, stable, serene, and filled with abundance but also has nasty storms, currents and waves that can crush weak ships. People who choose to live a smooth life

42

without too many contrasts often end up crushed to pieces by life's ocean when it doesn't play by their (often unconsciously created and unknown to them) rules. Life can and does throw you a multi-million dollar lottery ticket, a surprising but wanted baby, a divorce, deadly disease and a friend's passing all in the same breath, all on a sunny day. It can also provide long periods of stability that fools many into believing that they *"have life figured out"*. Trust me, they don't. The minute you admit life is out of your control and that all you control is your thoughts and actions, then you can consciously influence your own path.

What to do? The first step is to be realistic that life is an ocean and that the objective is to live with full freedom, passion and joy. This means building a ship (life) that is able to maneuver and even thrive in the turbulence. I believe the way to do that is to enjoy the voyage by living passionately in every moment. Realize that the contrasts are what make life so breathtaking. You couldn't enjoy the highs if there weren't lows. Life is also like the ocean in that it has cycles and seasons. I believe our passions and passion for life help us ride out the storms and enjoy the placid days equally. What will you do to prepare your life ship for the reality of life's ocean? Realizing it is a wild ride is half the battle!

--

"To be nobody but yourself in a world which is doing its best, night and day, to make you everybody else means to fight the hardest battle which any human being can fight; and never stop fighting." [1]

~ e.e. cummings, 1955

---

1   *http://www.quotegarden.com/be-self.html*

43

Chapter 2

Scarcity VS Abundance

"*I am told to just be myself, but as much as I have practiced the impression, I am still no good at it.*" [1]

~ Robert Brault

---

1 www.robertbrault.com

<u>Scarcity VS Abundance</u>

Courageous Authenticity Real Life Story: **My Little Voice**

Deep down inside I always knew that we were meant for more. Life just couldn't be as bland, passionless and structured as we had been taught in school. All these rules we were told we had to follow; who were they serving anyway? It just didn't jive with what my instincts were telling me.

I realized early on that I owe nothing to anyone other than to myself and to God and decided to follow my instincts. In life, I believe that everyone should ALWAYS follow their instincts, their "little voice", because that is where authenticity lies. When we pray, we talk to God; when we're inspired, it is God talking to us!

I haven't always had the courage to follow my little voice, but that day, towards the end of my university years, I did. I decided I would wake up when I pleased, do whatever it is I felt like doing, travel if I so wished, not pay taxes and not work for anyone or anything that would impose a set of rules upon me. I still did not know what I wanted to do... but at least I knew what I did not want to do... and I wasn't going to do it!

My life could have turned out even better had I followed my little voice more often, but I was well served from listening and acting upon it at least once, on that fateful day. As a result, I am if not financially free, definitely financially comfortable and flexible. I make my own schedule and focus on the things I want to focus on. I have learned many things and seen many places and most importantly, I have lived and felt FREE, rather than trapped. Freedom, it's beautiful and it keeps you young!

~ Billy K.

--

Myth: There's Not Enough To Go Around!

"When we give, we simply make room for more to come in. When we become deeply, authentically generous, it signals to our abundant universe that there is a conduit open to receive and distribute. We become part of the vital natural system." [1]

~ Lenedra J. Caroll

If an alien were to land on our planet and be locked in a lab with access to all our media but no contact with the real world, what perspective and impression of life on earth would it (not sure if aliens are male or female or both?) acquire? A very negative, frightening, powerless and insecure (#22 on the ES: Fear, Powerlessness, #21 Insecurity) view? A SCARCITY world view? The impact of a scarcity world view on the rest of us is the same; we are deeply influenced by it. Tragically, since most people have the "scarcity perspective" disease, we don't notice it as much. I cover the media and look at its broad impact in more detail in Chapter 10.

Taking From Others

Let's be authentically honest. Scarcity comes from fear of loss and fear of judgment because of that loss. It is a pervasive (across all life areas) perspective that there is not enough of anything and that life is hard.

Let me begin by defining what I mean by abundance. I mean having all the people, things and experiences that make our life feel full and magical. Abundance means not worrying about lack and feeling full no matter the outside situation or life circumstances (especially when they don't look or feel abundant) may be.

---

[1] http://www.successconsciousness.com/quotes/abundance.htm

It is very difficult or even impossible to really believe you can live life fully if you don't first and foremost believe in abundance. Why? Because you feel as if you're getting/experiencing something (relationship, success, joy, money) that removes it from someone else. A scarcity-based universe would be a sort of fixed pie (zero sum game) world. The universe is in constant expansion and constantly creates more. Scarcity is only in our minds and thoughts.

For example, after my partner Aida died almost three years ago, I basically did very little other than try to survive and make sense of the world. I didn't add much value to the world, and instead I was taking help wherever I could. Once I had worked through "enough" (we are never fully done grieving in my opinion) grief, I began doing what my heart said I should: help other people through my books, public speaking engagements and create men's and blended (men and women) circles.

Now I add a lot of new creative vehicles for others to expand their life. As such, the universe is sending me an absolutely limitless amount of co-creators who want to build a better world with me. All of this creation would not have occurred if I did not believe in an abundant universe. The universe is also sending me the financial rewards that go with changing many people's lives.

The Universe Is Fair

The universe is 100% fair. If you are not getting what you want, then you are not clear on what you want and the universe sends you confusion in return. Most people aren't asking clearly or they are not allowing the abundance to come. We allow abundance by raising our vibrational level (better feeling emotions on the ES, #1 to #7).

In an abundant universe mindset/belief, we shouldn't see others as competitors or enemies. We should see everyone as a possible collaborator in what we desire to create. When I negotiate with others I try to give them as much as I can so they will have "some skin in the game" with me. If they risk as much as I do, then they are as committed as I am. I currently have a business partner who I feel is not pulling her weight in a particular project. Being courageously authentic meant telling this person how I felt without being attached to what they would say or do with the information. My partner actually agreed with my point. In this case, I first focused on the fact that I see it as not fair that I am doing the lion's share of the work and yet we split the profits 50%/50%. By telling her about my perception (which may or not be true), I was authentic. In return, I learned where her motivations lay and I had no problem refocusing on my other projects.

--

Scarcity-Based Perspectives

In my opinion, most people have what I and many others call a scarcity perspective of the world and life. Many of our parents were around in World War II and developed a fear/scarcity based perspective which they passed on. The media is scarcity-focused as well. We have been programmed this way from a young age and for the most part we accept it as fact and rarely if ever question it. We are not told at what peril, that is left to our own investigations. Here are some examples.

"Money doesn't grow on trees."

"You need to go to school to have any hope of getting a good job and security."

Live It: Your Courageously Authentic Life

"Don't waste your food, there are children starving in Africa."

"There wasn't enough money to get you the present you REALLY wanted."

"The plant closed, Daddy lost his job, and we have to sell the house."

"Find a good woman/man soon, because it's impossible to meet anyone when you are over __ years old."

"Be careful when you cross the street."

"Don't talk to strangers."

"Take care!"

"Don't say what you think at work, because you may get fired!"

If we coldly look at these statements, they all come from a scarcity perspective. Yet many hold these as facts. They are not facts! These are perspectives based on the notion that there is limitation in the universe. This is not truth but the product of a fearful collective (media and societal) imagination. Under a scarcity perspective, if you get a good girlfriend/boyfriend, house, job, idea, then someone else is deprived of that resource or person.

> *The better we feel (appreciation/love/joy/empowerment/ freedom/passion) the more great people, experiences and prosperity come to us.*

The Universe Is Abundant

Being a card-carrying Law of Attraction practitioner, it is very clear to me now that in fact the universe is abundant and increasingly so, IF I think it is. The universe is abundant when we are in the higher emotional scale feelings (lower numbers like #1 Appreciation, Joy, Freedom, Empowerment and Love, #2 Passion. See Appendix 2 for the ES.). The better we feel, (#1 - #7 on the ES) the more great people, experiences and prosperity easily come to us.

More importantly perhaps is that we are creative in those emotions and can see the world in a much more neutral or beneficial way. We notice more things and as we appreciate them, we receive more. It is a self-reinforcing chain of emotions. I am sure you are very aware that when you are down, you are REALLY DOWN! Negative emotions at the bottom of the scale attract other similar events, thoughts and feelings (#22: Fear, Grief, Depression, Despair and Powerlessness).

I strongly believe that the universe is abundant and that a great idea I may have will actually create more where there was nothing before. However, when I'm immersed in the lower vibrations (higher numbers on the scale), I don't have access to creativity as I am attracting thoughts of fear, jealousy, anger, worry or self-blame.

Simply think of all the greatest inventions of our time from the automobile, refrigeration, air conditioning, planes, convenient health care, etc. These are all the idea of one person who felt that there was a better way. They were authentic in their feelings, they believed AND they acted on them. It is hard to argue that they didn't create abundance for all those who benefitted, much more so than if they had accepted the status quo and remained fearful and traditional in thinking.

51

Reframing Scarcity To Abundance

To test my idea that we are indoctrinated with a scarcity perspective from a young age, I have converted the previous scarcity/lack perspectives to abundant ones because I believe in them and strive to live my life in this mindset.

Scarcity: *"Money doesn't grow on trees."* Worry, #14 on the ES

This shows that money is rare, difficult to cultivate/attract.

Abundance: *"There is more than enough money for great people and ideas when I allow!"* Freedom, #1 on the ES

There is an unlimited supply of money (and all other forms of abundance) that goes to good ideas that come from the heart, not the head. Money is energy and most of us have a very negative view about money. Many see money as the root of all evil. It is not. Money is a tool and like any hammer it can build a home for orphans or bludgeon someone to death depending on the one who wields it. Money can help many people. Think of all the people you give jobs and profits to when you take a one week vacation. From the airline and staff of the airline and travel agency, to the rental car company and staff, the hotel company and staff and the countless meals and entertainment you consume on your trip.

> *Intuition told them to do something the banks and the masses considered "unsafe". What actually is unsafe is living a life that is not your own or trying to be something you are not.*

Scarcity: *"You need to go to school to have any hope of getting a good job and security."* Fear, #22 on the ES

Any either/or statements that are black and white like this one are defacto incorrect as the world has many shades of gray.

Yes, many people have great jobs and great educations. But is the education really causing the great job? Could there be personal factors like perseverance, flexible thinking, and ability to collaborate that influence success? Absolutely! Both Bill Gates and Steve Jobs were college dropouts as are many creative and visionary internet/rap/movie-making millionaires!

Abundance: "What creates security is passion for what you do, and the fact you know you are unique and can tap that uniqueness to help the world." Passion, #2 on the ES

No one gets to be successful unless they are able to tap directly into their heart (their emotional compass) for inspiration. Great ideas are born from great emotions and great passion to do better and risk it all! Most entrepreneurs credit their "little voice", their intuition that told them to do something that the banks and the masses would consider unsafe. What I believe to be the truly unsafe way, is to live a life that is not your own or try to be something you are not (usually something we think others want us to be). That never works as the vibration is inauthentic, scattered, and has no lasting power.

--

Scarcity: *"Don't waste your food, there are children starving in Africa."* Worry, #14 on the ES

There is food and you must not waste it as it is scarce. Children starving is also scarcity thinking. The fact is that in most starving and poor countries people are much happier than in our successful (financially yes, morally corrupt/bankrupt) western societies.

Live It: Your Courageously Authentic Life

Abundance: *"Take what you can eat and there will be plenty for tomorrow."* Empowerment, #1 on the ES

Once we trust that the universe is abundant, we don't worry as much about tomorrow. We enjoy living in the moment, which can be seen as imprudent by society, as we must plan for a dangerous (Fear, #22 on the ES) future.

> **Begin accepting the reality that NOT everyone will love or like you but that's okay, because you don't like or love everyone else either.**

Scarcity: *"There's not enough money to get you the gift you really wanted."* Worry, #14 on the ES

Again, money is a very rare and limited commodity and we don't have enough.

Abundance: *"We gave you this gift which comes from love and joy."* Love and Joy, #1 on the ES

Children don't need to be told of lack and limitation. They see it being modeled all around them anyway and it's burnt into their brains at a young age. Children need to be shown that the world is abundant, safe, fun and that love is the most important thing, above ALL ELSE.

--

Scarcity: *"The plant closed, Daddy lost his job, and we have to sell the house."* Fear, #22 on the ES

This may be true but the real truth may be that Daddy was too lazy to upgrade his skills and counted on being paid a salary based on the power of someone else (a union). Or maybe Daddy is not a very good money manager and has a gambling/alcohol addiction.

Abundance: *"The plant closed, Daddy lost his job and now he gets to do what he really wants, and we are also moving to make a new start!"* Empowerment, #1 on the ES

Kids are smart and they can handle the truth better than adults. They understand and relate to authenticity.

Don't be nice, be authentic!

--

Scarcity: *"Find a good woman/man soon since it's impossible to meet anyone when you are over ..."* Worry, #14 on the ES

The false assumption underlying this example is that we get older and less attractive and marketable. This may be true ONLY if all that matters is appearance (this belief is ego based). The fact is that many of us like fine wines do get better with age. With the proper nutrition and exercise our bodies can retain 90% of their youthful vitality. You may want to consult my book, *"Killing Yourself With Your Fork?!*[1]*"* for more information on increasing your vitality.

Abundance: *"The perfect person is out there for you and will be there when you allow the time and space for them and really like and embrace your authentic, most brilliant self."* Freedom, #1 on the ES

---

1   http://bookstore.iuniverse.com/Products/SKU-000124334/Killing-Yourself-with-your-fork.aspx

Live It: Your Courageously Authentic Life

Authenticity is sexy, hot and engaging. <u>Worst case scenario:</u> those around you who insist on wearing masks will be confronted and entertained. <u>Best case scenario:</u> you start attracting people who really like you for who you are and want to build a life with you. It all begins with accepting and learning to love yourself (start with "like" if "love" is too strong!). Once you do, you start being that person and accepting that not everyone will love or like you but that's okay, because you don't like or love everyone else either! My vision wall encourages me: *"Don't be nice, be authentic!"*

--

<u>Scarcity:</u> *"Be careful when you cross the street."* Worry, #14 on the ES

Here, the perspective is that the world is a very dangerous place and we must continuously be vigilant or we will get hurt or worse, die! Did you know that humans are the only animals on earth that have the cognitive ability (and curse) of worrying about death? Almost from the moment we are born we are sent fearful messages about dying. I say curse because, as they say, *"death and taxes are the only two certainties in this life."* Worrying about death (since death is a terminal condition all humans go through) actually brings it on as worry creates cancer in the body as does any extended bouts of negative emotions. The emotions above #8, boredom, are all healing and rejuvenating.

--

<u>Abundance:</u> *"Have a blast out there!"* Empowerment and Freedom, #1 on the ES

In this perspective, life is seen as fun and the risk is in having too little fun and playfulness. The emotion here is joy #1 and passion #2 on the ES. It also envisions and creates the world as a fun and exciting adventure. Life is a fun and exciting adventure IF and ONLY <u>IF</u> you believe it is.

Remember Henry Ford said: *"Whether you think you can or can't, you're right!"*

--

<u>Scarcity:</u> *"Don't talk to strangers."* Fear, #22 on the ES

The underlying meaning of this message is that strangers are dangerous and fearful. They may hurt, kill or steal from us and should be avoided. This is definitely the product of fear and insurance companies and lawyers are the only ones benefitting from it. However, fear is more dangerous than that. It stifles and kills all creativity and free thinking. Remember, good decisions can NEVER come from negative emotions (below #7 on the ES). I generally attempt to avoid making decisions on those days.

<u>Abundance:</u> *"The world is your family/playground!"* Freedom, #1 on the ES

I created this analogy four years ago at a seminar. In it, there is love and appreciation and freedom and all are #1 on the ES. What kind of experience do you think this person will have out in the world by embracing everything around them? They will have great experiences all the time and in fact, others will be attracted to them for their fearless and loving nature. Love attracts love, fear attracts fear. It's that simple.

If you immediately thought, *"Yes, but someone may take advantage of you if you are nice!"*, this is a worried (#14 on the ES) thought and it is true. Some may take advantage. This is where having strong, authentic and meaningful personal boundaries will allow you to decide when someone has crossed the line. I find that I feel much better trusting everyone until proven wrong (abundance) than believing I only give trust after it's earned (scarcity and fear). Yes, I do get taken some times, but that's just part of life and it's never about me, it's about them.

--

> *We all have the power to change our life in one second by making a powerful, aligned, with our heart (not head) decision.*

Scarcity: *"Take care!"* Fear, #22 on the ES

This is laced with fear that the world is dangerous and you must be careful or get hurt or worse (die). I always have fun with this one when people say it to me. I usually, say back to them, *"Find something and take care of it!"* A statement like "take care" would be perfect if one was about to leave on a long mysterious journey fraught with real danger, but not for a daily commute to school or work.

Abundance: "Have an adventurous, exciting and empowering day!" Passion and Empowerment, #2, and #1 on the ES

The power of those words is incredible! They assume again that great things will happen, and they will! It's a wonderful way to be in the world.

--

<u>Scarcity:</u> *"Don't say what you think at work, because you may get fired."* Fear, #22 on the ES

Be inauthentic, put on a mask and maybe you get to keep your job, if you are lucky! Notice that the scarcity perspective also has powerlessness (#22 on the ES) almost automatically baked in: *"It's not your fault, the world is scarce. You are experiencing that reality."* I don't buy it for one second. We all have the power to change our life in one second by making a powerful, aligned with our heart (not head) decision. Most people give away that power as they somehow feel unworthy (#21 on the ES) or fearful that they might misuse it. Most of my clients say their #1 barrier to success is themselves.

<u>Abundance:</u> *"Be your true (authentic) self at work!"* Freedom, #1 on the ES

They will either love you and embrace your uniqueness, perspective and talents, or they will fire you because you don't fit. However, a positive new world will await you along with an opportunity to find a more authentic job or calling. It takes tremendous courage to be authentic and as such the payoff for being that way is commensurately massive. The universe sends you a positive response.

> ***Life and the universe IS abundant, look at stars, billions of them, flowers in a field, unlimited.***

--

Live It: Your Courageously Authentic Life

Live It! Activity #7: Please list three of your current scarcity perspectives. Then reframe them with an abundance perspective. I give you an example from my life.

Scarcity: *"There aren't many partners that would be a match for me."*

Abundance: *"All I need is ONE good person, just one! Let's have fun out there!"*

Scarcity Perspective	Abundance Perspective
1. _____	_____
2. _____	_____
3. _____	_____

I challenge you to keep looking at your prominent thoughts. Are they from scarcity (probably) or abundance (hopefully)? Remember the higher up the ES scale you are numerically and emotionally, the greater the chance of your seeing the world as abundant. It IS abundant. Look at the stars, billions of them; flowers in a field, unlimited. If nature is unlimited why would we be limited? We are part of nature, and not above it, as most foolishly believe.

You are also abundant with hopes, dreams, aspirations, talents and love. If those are NOT your defacto emotions, chances are, you are living in some areas (perhaps even all) with less integrity and authenticity. Check in with your heart. What does it long for? What does it cherish? If you won the lottery what would you still do? Start doing more of that. There's no time like the present. What if you die tonight?

In my case if I won the lottery, I would probably keep teaching but open my own school. I would still coach, speak, write and run men's and blended circles. I would travel the world more as it feeds my soul and freedom (#1 on the ES) which is one of my top values. So you can see I'm living my life purpose. It feels great! Are you living your purpose? How do you know? We will create your life purpose in Chapter 8.

--

Useful Ways To Begin Practicing Abundant Thinking

1. Decide and commit immediately to <u>start thinking abundant thoughts and then do it</u>. I have a client who created a jar and puts a penny in the jar for every negative thought. She is amazed at how full the jar is! Or put a penny for every positive thought you have (a forced easy saving method, and you could spend the savings on something nice, like a trip!)

2. Actually count (and record/journal) your numerous blessings right now, and start being grateful (Appreciation is #1 on the ES) for all the amazing things, people and experiences in your life. Be grateful for your body and health.

3. Stop thinking about what you believe you DON'T have. Instead, focus on creating the circumstances that you DO want. Develop your passions, interests, knowledge, and skills in areas that will help you achieve more.

4. Replace *"could've"*, "should've" and *"would've"* with *"I want"* or "I *will soon have"*. Begin visualizing and feeling what it will be like to have it (tell your mind that the "How" is not your responsibility).

5. <u>Don't feel guilty</u> (Guilt, #21 on the ES) for wanting / desiring. It is your personal choice to strive for happiness for yourself and others.

6. <u>You can want, but NEVER create specific expectations.</u> Having expectations leads to disappointment. Be committed but not attached to a particular result or outcome.

For more abundance, give more and expect less from life.

---

7. Better yet, create <u>zero expectations</u> of what you will receive. Do not automatically assume that you will receive anything. Just know that anything and everything is possible and invite that abundance into your life. Be abundant with others; be appreciative, passionate, free and loving. These are all the ultimate feel-good emotions.

8. <u>Be mentally prepared (but not focused on) for worst case scenarios.</u> Know that in the right emotional state you can and will easily handle anything and everything the world (recall, it's like an ocean) will throw at you. Think positively about receiving what you want, but do not Live It as read. If you meet your goals, it will add to the happiness you already enjoy. If not, it doesn't matter because <u>you are happy with what you already have.</u>

9. <u>Eliminate thinking the world owes you a living and that you deserve to</u> receive what you want. Everything you receive in life is a gift. The world doesn't owe you anything, but its abundance is capable of giving you anything and everything you desire, when you play full out.

10. <u>Remember the universe is fair.</u> You must give to receive BUT never give EXPECTING to receive. Give more, expect less.

> ### *PERFECTIONISM equals and leads to PARALYSIS*

11. <u>Stop feeling cheated and like a victim</u>. (Powerlessness, #22 on the ES) This is the scarcity perspective. Take control and responsibility of your life and by extension your own happiness.

12. <u>Know that your past does not equal your future and your current</u> unfavorable situation does not have to last if YOU choose to make it better. You are not your condition or circumstances, but <u>YOU ARE your thoughts</u>. Take 100% responsibility that your past thoughts and choices have lead you exactly to where you are. Once you do, you will feel in control of (and love) your life (Empowerment, #1 on the ES).

13. <u>Accept that you will make mistakes.</u> PERFECTIONISM equals and leads to PARALYSIS. Don't beat yourself up when you do, regard mistakes as moments on your learning curve that will help take you to new heights. Learn from them and move on. Our hardest knocks teach us our most important lessons in life. We learn many more lessons from our failures than our successes. Ask any sports team or Olympic athlete!

14. <u>Think of a physical reminder that will help you keep your thoughts on track.</u> Every time you feel you are drifting back to thoughts of scarcity, perform your little physical action to realign yourself with abundance. You could click your fingers, snap a rubber band on your wrist, or simply join your thumb to your forefinger as people do in meditation.

15. <u>Develop a mantra that you repeat every morning and evening or whenever you need a boost</u>. An example I use is, *"Every day and in every way the universe gives me more than I need!"*

"Not what we have, but what we enjoy, constitutes our abundance." [1]

~ Epicurus

---

1   http://gettingtozen.com/2011/08/your-thoughts-dictate-your-action/

Chapter 3

Tripping on STUMPS

"Be who you are and say what you feel, because those who mind don't matter and those who matter don't mind." [1]

~ Dr. Seuss

1   http://www.quotegarden.com/be-self.html

Tripping on STUMPS

Courageous Authenticity Real Life Story: Sending My Family to Jail for Sexual Abuse.

"Where do I start ... expressing my thoughts and feelings of the sexual abuse I have endured... the effects, I am sure are still with me to this day. I'm not sure who will read my story. If anyone that knows me reads this, I would say to them, "This is my story; this is who I am and why I am the way I am."

My abusers: Nine relatives, uncles and cousins. I was abused as far back as I can remember. Sleepless nights became a normal routine for me. Always too terrified to sleep, I usually slept underneath my bed. At the age of seven, I endured three reconstructive operations on my inner reproductive system from the abuse I endured. On many occasions I was sexually abused while my parents were home. I tried telling my parents before the age of twelve on many occasions but my parents were always too intoxicated and disinterested. They knew what was going on, but were cowards.

The abuse stopped when I was twelve. That day I got off the school bus and I saw that I was being followed by one of my relatives. I ran as fast as I could. He caught me and pulled me into a forest area where he held me down to the ground. I screamed and kicked him. He punched me a few times, knocked out my front teeth, as he tried to take off my clothes. I continued to scream. Somehow I was able to free myself. I ran home. He followed me. My parents were home. He came in my house yelling, "Where's Cindy, she needs to come with me somewhere!" I came to the door and screamed at him saying, "Get out, you are never touching me again." My parents listened and said nothing. I ran to my next door neighbour's house and called the police.

I disclosed to the police about all my abusers. Charges were laid. My parents demanded that I drop the charges. I refused. While attending court for six months, hearing death threats from my relatives became a normal routine. I was removed from my home by the police and I never returned to that home again. I went to court alone. All my relatives were charged. I was never sexually abused again.

Today I am extremely happy, attained two university degrees, have two well-adjusted, intelligent and loving creative teenage children. I have a man who loves me deeply for all of who I am. I am an accomplished leader in my workplace and would select my job as a palliative care nurse above ANY SUM OF MONEY. I have the career I always dreamed about. I choose to love every second of my life and take nothing for granted.

~ Cindy O.

--

Meet Your STUMPS

There are powerful forces conspiring to stop you from Living It! They will stop at nothing to scare you, bully you and discredit and undermine all your efforts to live your most courageously authentic life. They will lie, cheat, manipulate and generally keep you small. They definitely come from a SCARCITY perspective.

Unfortunately for you and me, even if we isolate ourselves from the outside world these forces will not disappear. For as we know, *"wherever you go there you are!"* Wherever you go your mind is there with you. In this chapter, we will discover your STUMPS and provide tools to deal with and manage them. Although there ARE external forces stopping authenticity they pale in comparison to the greatest negative forces of them all, our inner mind committee of STUMPS.

These forces are in our heads, they are our own negative, self-limiting STUMPS!

STUMPS

Saboteur
Trickster
U (in you)
Most
Pathetic
Self

I have created and now consistently use the term Saboteur/ Trickster Most Pathetic Self to designate your most negative/pathetic voice. For ease of reading I have created the acronym, STUMPS, as these STMPS are part of "U"! Like tree stumps they will always block and trip you up, if you're not aware. Awareness is power against your nasty STUMPS. I've heard STUMPS also described as "negative inner voice", "inner critic", "inner committee" and "gremlin" (not the cute furry ones but the nasty monstrous ones!). Perhaps you know others.

> **Be aware that where you are in your life is a direct reflection of HOW MUCH you listen to your STUMPS.**

Here's a good definition from another coach, Andrea Owen:

"The inner critic or "gremlin" is the negative voice that can range from very negative self-criticism to simply disempowering. There is no way to completely turn off your inner critic voice, but doing work around it and managing it can be enormously helpful." [1]

---

1   Article source: http://EzineArticles.com/6296485

A second description from another coach, Alana Tobin [1]:

"Gremlin is a well known term in coaching circles representing the 'inner critic,' a personification of the negative inner voice. Gremlins are conceived through the passing along of negative or self defeating messages which have been internalized throughout life. Well meaning parents, teachers, siblings and associates who like ourselves, are challenged intermittently with the voices of the gremlin have (unconsciously) passed these along. When the voice of the gremlin overpowers our authentic voice (Most Brilliant Self FM), it can feel difficult to go after what we most desire, as we become plagued by self doubt, fear, or feelings of low esteem.

Gremlins are discouraging, and can easily convince us that we are not capable or worthy of being, having, or doing what we desire to experience in life. At times, it may appear as though there are insurmountable obstacles blocking us from realizing our goals, such as: writing that book, starting a new business, losing weight, healing a relationship, etc.

Gremlins may discourage you from speaking up for yourself, or act to obscure your own needs in favor of others'. Gremlins also nurture feelings of low self esteem, which can prevent you from taking advantage of opportunities. Familiar messages such as "I'm not good enough" or "I can't, shouldn't or won't succeed" are expressions of the gremlin. Gremlins make it very easy to envision a "worst case scenario" for every situation."

Your STUMPS may tell you, *"No wonder you have no money, you're a loser!"*, or something worse! It is the conglomeration of all the worst things you ever heard from others or thought about yourself. It limits you and keeps you small. Be careful, he/she is just as smart as you and is infinitely crafty (a trickster tricks you!).

It always lies and says, *"This horrible thing will happen if...."*

---

1 *http://friendfinder.com/intgroups.aa167/tyadmin/acprint_admin_article.html*

Live It: Your Courageously Authentic Life

Amazingly, most people never question its logic or agenda as they think it is themselves talking (and not a scared and immature part of themselves). Once you do, they adapt and re-spawn in an infinitely creative and different form (like gremlins)! Be aware that where you are in your life is a direct reflection of HOW MUCH you listen to your STUMPS. They are usually extreme.

Example: *"You will always fail miserably!"*

They have zero subtlety! In the above example the word "always" gives it away. STUMPS conversations become easier to identify and counteract or ignore when we are on the lookout for the words "always" and "never". So now that you know your STUMPS, realize that ALL your self-sabotage emanates from it. It can't help it. The fact is our brains and subconscious minds need to constantly be at work and think something, anything really. In the next section I will share tools to manage the STUMPS, as they can never be completely eradicated (while you're brain is working you have a STUMPS).

> **If your STUMPS puts you at ease about how prevalent it is, it has won, because then it can hide.**

If you don't give your mind productive, life affirming, self-promoting work, it will do destructive work. They (STUMPS thoughts) run wildly about causing havoc. They are wild and untrained like unruly teenagers before they are drafted into the army or sent to boarding school. Your job is to be the stern adult to rebuke, question or ignore them regularly. How? Begin by noticing your STUMPS.

They usually have one of only three or four broken record conversations for you, such as:

"You've failed at this before, why would things be different now?"

"You don't deserve it!" or "You're not able to!"

"Why bother, it never works!"

"You can't do it, don't even try, it's/you're way too _____ (insert the following: big, ambitious, exciting, aggressive, unrealistic, optimistic, early, late, different, young, old, etc. ad nauseum).

As you can see they have a complete and convincing arsenal of lies and half truths. Now you know. Be vigilant. But follow your idea/intuition anyway!

--

Live It! Activity #8: What are your top five most common STUMPS thought patterns? List them below:

1. _____

2. _____

3. _____

4. _____

5. _____

What impact on your life have these (often subconscious) limiting thoughts had? Be honest and authentic here! This for you, no one else!_____
_____

--

Live It: Your Courageously Authentic Life

Stumps Hate Mind Gyms!

Don't think your STUMPS is happy to be focused on or asked to improve by doing exercises aimed at minimizing it. It will quite brazenly and literally sabotage your efforts and STUMPS you! I'll bet you right now yours might be saying, "*I don't have a STUMPS*" or "*I control mine really well!*" or more subtle "*I choose when I want to be STUMPSed!*" The minute it puts you at ease about how nasty, prevalent or wrong it is, it has won.

The flip side (and equally as powerful cousin) of your STUMPS is your *"Most Brilliant Self"* or *"Most Authentic Self!"* This is who we need to always strive to be.

--

John Kehoe[1] in "Mind Power For the 21st Century" covers four ways that we can manage the negatives that our STUMPS consistently beat us up with. The key thing I have found implementing these four techniques is to try them out until you find which ones work best for you and/or in different situations.

Four Ways To Deal With STUMPS Negative Thoughts

1. <u>Cut it off.</u> Whenever you have a negative thought you replace it with any (unconnected) thought at all, skiing, shopping, weather, anything! All you are doing here is acting like you do with a pesky child who keeps hounding you about buying him/her a toy, you change the subject. Often they don't even notice as they are so busy with their one track negative focus.

2. <u>Observe it, as a third party.</u> <u>To eliminate: Negatives ONLY</u> have power over you when <u>you</u> REACT to them. If you choose not to engage, it will lose interest and find other ways to heckle you. Once you realize this it's very liberating! Negatives get their power FROM you. If you fail to react they have no power over you." Tell yourself, "*Oh, there you are, how interesting, what*

1   Kehoe, John, Mind Power for the 21st Century, Zoetic

are you saying again, right." Curiosity kills them as it shines a light and asks them to clarify. The key is to not invest a lot of energy on them! The more thought and energy you give them the more real and dangerous they become.

3. Expand them to ridiculousness. Take it to the absurd! It needs to get to the point where you laugh.

    Example: You are worried about a project you are late completing and your STUMPS chimes in, *"You screw up, and you'll get in so much trouble!"* Before, you would have jumped on the bandwagon and agreed with your STUMPS and started coming up with much worse scenarios to beat yourself up with.

    Now though, you go on the offensive and expand its comment to ridiculousness: *"Absolutely I'll be in trouble. Not only will I get in trouble, but I'm probably going to be suspended and then fired! Then to make it worse, I'll get all stressed about it and get cancer and lose all my limbs. Then I'll just be a stump myself; wow life will be bad!"* You need a good sense of humor as they are so negative!

4. Counteract the negative with the exact opposite. For example, if your STUMPS tell you, *"You're ugly!"* Remind yourself of all the times people have told you how attractive you are. Such as, *"Actually, John Smith at the grocery store commented on how fit I looked and asked me out Saturday!"* Facts and third party corroboration really stifle them!

--

Live It! Activity #9: Go over your MOST PREVALENT negative self-talk. Which of the above feels like it would work best for you? Write it down and look out for it. I extensively use Cut It Off (#1) and Counteract with the exact opposite (#4). <u>I can tell you that after a while of doing this regularly your STUMPS will rarely get to you for any extended periods!</u>

--

Trickster and No Treats

John Kehoe describes what I call the STUMPS as the *"Great Trickster"*, which describes the incessant wasted, negative chatter (low emotions such as Worry, Guilt and Fear, all are #20 and lower on the ES). We all have the negative chatter. We can never fully eradicate it! Even you! He describes how the masses are living unconscious lives playing constant mind games with themselves that lead nowhere.

I describe it as spinning your wheels while you spin the steering wheel while driving! You can't move in any direction with speed or purpose with a crazy trickster at the helm constantly jamming your throttle (mind energy) full out and then shifting from "D" to "R" (D = progressing forward and growing at full speed and R is when we shut down all creativity due to fear.)

> *"Let go of "uncontrollables" like the economy, weather, spouse, family. Your time and energy is now permanent free to resolve only WHAT YOU CAN CONTROL →YOU and your actions, and who you are being.*

The (untrained) mind <u>constantly ruminates over negatives</u> wasting precious mind power going upstream (this is an Abraham

Hicks term meaning against the flow of the river of abundance), getting self-upset! Then we stay in one frustrated/angry/depressed state and give up!

Example: Assume you have someone who said something negative to you and you didn't resolve it. You latch onto it and you let it ruin your day. You begin imagining what you will say to that person, and how they will reply. *"They'll say this, and I'll say that, then what about this, and what about that? I'll say that, then he'll say that, but I'll say that, that'll get him! But what if he says this? Then I'll say that, or maybe this!"*

You go back and forth with your own mind until you have a headache, are exhausted, frustrated and worried, and nothing is resolved. Your STUMPS just had a battle with you and won. You just beat yourself up creating a fictional conversation that probably will never happen. If it does happen, it is because you are focusing on it ! It is making you crazy and is a great example of an untrained mind. A trained mind would say, *"There's not much I can do without speaking to that person and I will be present and we can resolve it then. Now I will enjoy the rest of this glorious spring day."*

The above illustrates the definition of suffering which I find helps me to determine where to invest my mind's emotional energy. It may seem simple but it is very true and powerful once you begin applying it to every time you are suffering. It works.

> *"The average person has three negative thoughts per second!"*

Maintaining Powerful Brain Power

Any tool that helps me to conserve critical positive emotional states and brain power is very important. When we vibrate at the higher vibrations we are aligned and optimally creative. I really like to create! Think about how many thoughts you have in a day, the actual number is somewhere between 12,000 and 60,000 a day.

"A well-known author was quoted as saying that 'The average person has 60,000 thoughts per day and of these more than 80% are negative."

So let's split the difference and suggest about 36,000 thoughts in a day. If only 50% are negative, that's 18,000 negative thoughts a day. Let's say we are awake sixteen hours and sleep eight hours. That's 18000/16 = 1125 negative thoughts per hour. That's 188 negative thoughts per minute. That's three Negative thoughts per second. If you can increase that to two positives and one negative per second that gives you 50% more positive thoughts. Imagine what you can and will attract! Like attracts like.

As previously mentioned, I had a client once who had a large jar in the kitchen and every time she had a negative thought, she would put a penny in the jar. She had a very good understanding of how many negative thoughts she had as the jar quickly filled up.

> ***Paradoxically, giving up "apparent" control gives you actual/real control.***

Boundaries And Suffering

- Our individual preferences create our boundaries (Example: I prefer alternative rock to pop.)

- Those with strong boundaries (preferences) are more resilient and handle stress better.

- If you prefer jazz to rock or hiking to cycling, this creates a strong personal boundary around you AND ALLOWS YOU to more easily say yes and no.

Uncontrollables

Weather, economy, boss, other people. What else?

Stress

- Holes in our boundaries MISLEAD us to think SOMETHING or SOMEONE is controllable by us, but this is IMPOSSIBLE!

- Strong boundaries (reinforced by clear preferences) allow stress and negative emotions from others to simply bounce off.

Definition of Suffering

The definition of suffering = "Is worrying about things you don't and can't control."   Examples of what you CAN'T control [1] include but are not limited to the economy, the weather, your boss, spouse, etc.

Once you let go of these uncontrollables, your time and energy is free to resolve what you CAN CONTROL. What you CAN control is YOU and your actions and who you are being! (This is what all higher spiritual practices suggest).

--

Paradoxically, giving up apparent control of what is outside yourself gives you actual/real control of what you do, think or say, and who you are BEING (Inner World).

---

1   *D'Angelo, David, Deep Inner Game*

--

Implement ONLY this one change and your quality of life will dramatically improve. As a bonus, you will also receive all of the positive events and people that arrive in your experience, because you are present and not worrying about the past or the future, free to enjoy the present moment. The amount of pennies I find (apparently a very positive event, I love it!) is due to my being present and aware of my environment at most times (NOT stressed, but PRESENT). This becomes an extremely amazing way to live as everything is brighter and more defined. It's as if you literally look at the world with rose colored glasses and get out of your head and into your heart.

Live It! Activity #10: Make a list of ten things that you will stop worrying about AT THIS VERY SECOND (because they are out of your control and you can't control them anyway!):

_____	_____
_____	_____
_____	_____
_____	_____
_____	_____

In conclusion, your STUMPS needs to be witnessed, identified, understood and dealt with so its impact can be managed (reduced).

--

"I'm perfect in my imperfections, happy in my pain, strong in my weakness and beautiful in my own way cause I'm me." [1]

~ Unknown

---

[1] www.searchquotes.com/search/Being_true_to_yourself

Chapter 4

Women Living It!

"Always be a first-rate version of yourself, instead of a second-rate version of somebody else." [1]

~ Judy Garland

1   http://www.quotegarden.com/be-self.html

Women Living It!

A Woman Empowered!

I was, in the past blind to the power of my own self, mainly because I truly didn't have the faith or belief that I was fully capable of creating my own life. I was raised with the mentality to work hard and be successful, but the problem was I wasn't taught to explore what I wanted. Just over 8 weeks ago I accepted an experience that was really out of the box for me. To discover the amazing work of mind power, Law of Attraction, inner world and outer world connection and the most exciting thing of all, learning that I have to ability to create my own reality. I am 19 years old.

Once I learned of these teachings I realized it's not as foreign to me as I thought it was. For example, my own natural self was, in the past, replacing negative thoughts with positive, verbally assuring myself that a situation will be successful, and visualizing what I want in life. But I didn't know what these thoughts inside me were, what they were called, how to use them, and most importantly how powerful they truly are. After learning of these extraordinary teachings, it brought all the pieces together. It turned up the power to such an unbelievable level of ability in myself.

Now life is different:

- *I've readjusted my long term goals with things I LOVE and truly WANT*

- *I only do things that make me feel so happy while doing them, and I strive to do them as much as I can*

- *I dream BIG , visualize BIG and will live BIG*

"Life is such an amazing journey and HAPPINESS is one of the most important aspects of life."

~ Kristi G.

--

Male Feminine & Female Masculine

I'm a man (obviously!) and that definitely alters and colours my perspective of life. It also impacts the whole thesis of Live It! as my biases as a man are present. I strongly believe the principles in this book are universal to both men and women. Whether you are a man or a woman, living the best life that you can is not only recommended, it is your duty to yourself and the world!

> ***All men possess many aspects that are traditionally held as "feminine"***

All men and women regardless of background, race or culture (or any and all other economic, socioeconomic and psychographic differences) have aspects that are both masculine and feminine. In my particular case, I have many traditional masculine traits such as natural assertiveness, competitiveness, aggression, "take-charge" attitude, etc. All men also possess many aspects that are traditionally held as feminine. Examples include intuition, empathy, nurturing, crying at sad movies, listening and overall spacial and personal emotional management characteristics. These are usually found at generally higher levels in women. If you are a woman, you still have many of both masculine and feminine aspects and should not discount "Live It!" and courageous authenticity as the primary domain of men.

Women: More Courageous Than Men

I also believe that in many ways women are much more courageous than men (a fact rarely celebrated in "big acts of courage/ once in a lifetime" mass media). Courage means hanging in there day after day, even when all exterior circumstances and results appear to be negative and against you. One of the most painful physical ailments is kidney stones which are excruciating. The only other physical experience often compared with the extent of that pain is childbirth. Having children multiple times is an incredibly difficult and courageous thing to do. Adding the commitment of a minimum of 18 years as a child's primary caregiver is even more challenging.

> *"You miss 100% of the shots you don't take."*
> *~ Wayne Gretsky*

Women Ask 9 Times Less Than Men

There was a study that was conducted about seven years ago that posited that women NEGOTIATE FOR WHAT THEY WANT from two to nine TIMES LESS OFTEN than men do!

"Women are much less likely than men to ask for what they want and to use negotiation as a tool to promote their own ambitions or desires. Sara interviewed nearly 100 people all over the country—both men and women—and found the same thing. Men use negotiation to get ahead and get what they want between two and nine times as often as women do." [1]

To me, this is very powerful evidence that women NEED to be more assertive, to ask for what they want and start living it!

---

[1] http://www.womendontask.com/questions.html

Wayne Gretzky (Hockey Hall of Famer widely considered one of the best players ever) said, *"You miss 100% of the shots you don't take."* It seems so obvious in sports but is completely applicable to our lives. What are the devastating and life limiting side effects of NOT taking shots?

--

The Costs of Not Taking A Shot

1. You miss all the opportunities (because you chose not to take a shot) and let fear win.

2. You miss the learning and growth of trying, failing and persevering to take shots.

3. Your ego gets to smugly hide behind a carefully crafted lifelong sabotaging lie: "If I did try I would succeed! But I didn't so I didn't fail." NOT giving your all is always failure.

4. The world doesn't get the benefit of your shot, whatever impact it might have, although it is certainly more than not doing anything.

5. You don't inspire anyone else to take shots around you. Those who regularly go for it inspire others by their actions (the main concept in Live It!).

"Be the change you want to see in the world."

~ **Gandhi**

--

What You Want Is Your Business

Women want and desire different things than men do. What you want to take, however, is not relative to the scope of Live It! It's your job to figure out what you want and desire, and to then authentically and courageously ask for it or do what it takes to get it. The next few chapters will allow you to determine exactly what you want. Clarity is powerful.

> *Their authentic courage to do what they thought, felt and knew was right despite all resistance, judgment and even death is powerfully inspiring.*

Incredibly Successful Women Set The Bar High

Look at incredibly successful women in history who had the gift or inspiration of authentic courage and lived how they wanted to. The world was/is much better for their inspired vision and efforts that changed the course of history FOR THE BETTER.

Examples:

Joan of Arc: Led the French to victory against the English.

The Witches of Salem: All burnt at the stake for their beliefs and lifestyle.

Amelia Earhart: Intrepid woman who circumnavigated the world, flying.

Madame Curie: A physicist who discovered the chemicals radium and polonium and won a Nobel Prize.

Mother Teresa: Helped millions of children and the ill in Calcutta, India.

<u>Rosa Parks:</u> American Black rights leader who refused to give up her seat to a white man.

<u>Oprah Winfrey:</u> The iconic TV star and producer who continues to inspire the world.

There are millions of other unsung heroes who toiled daily to help or create and support families.

All of these women have many things in common, but the greatest to me is their *<u>authentic courage to do what they thought, felt and knew was right despite all resistance, judgment and even death.</u>*

A person who is authentic has a power and presence that transcends EVERY conceivable traditional measure of attractiveness

---

Leading a life of courageous authenticity is a tremendous act and a most difficult, but ultimately immeasurably rewarding choice. <u>Will you have that courage?</u> In my deepest heart I hope so, for the sake of yourself and the bettered world we will experience. Don't waste this life, because none of us get a "redo". As I always tell my clients:

"This is not a Practice Life!"

<u>My personal experience:</u> As an evolved and self-assured, open to life and living man, I am immediately and powerfully attracted to a woman who is courageously authentic in her communication and behavior, and who is consistently true to herself (I don't think we can ultimately ever be 100% transparent). Forget any notion of physical beauty for a moment. A person who is authentic has a power and presence that transcends EVERY conceivable traditional measure of attractiveness.

Being real and authentic is so rare in this superficial world. This is why it is immensely attractive and contributes to animal magnetism. So many want to be themselves but are afraid of judgment and criticism. Look at most Hollywood movie scripts: many involve the main character(s) choosing to be their real selves, no matter what. If the people around you don't like your authentic self, it is THEIR PROBLEM (they may be inauthentic or have very different values than you do). I suggest you begin surrounding yourself with people who are authentic.

Once you begin living this authenticity, all will take care of itself as inauthentic relationships fall by the wayside and are replaced with authentic and much more satisfying ones. You don't even have to actively work on this as your vibration [1] (Universal Manager) takes care of it.

> **Whenever you are angry, depressed, or frustrated, you are in the lower (fear) quadrant.**

Higher And Lower Feminine

I'd like to take a moment to go over a diagram that I have found exceedingly useful for both men and women. I have included The Masculine and Feminine diagram in Appendix 4 [2].

Note: This diagram is Feminine and Masculine and NOT women and men.

When coming from unconscious fear or deprivation,

---

[1] *All things in the universe are vibration.Energy, sound, light can all be broken down into waves of vibration. Our vibration is what people are drawn to or repulsed by. By choosing to be your authentic self your vibration becomes clean and strong.*

[2] *Glover, Robert, No More Mr. Nice Guy, Copyright 2000*

Feminine's negatives are:

- Helpless (feels powerless and worthless, both #22 on the ES)

- Feels Victimized (actively ignores or gives away any power we may actually have)

- Personalizes (feels everything is done to us or is about us)

- Resentful (Revenge is #18 on the ES)

- Needy (because of learned helplessness)

- Feels Trapped (without courageously accessing and using our personal power we feel and stay trapped)

- Passive-Aggressive (not assertive in voicing our thoughts, preferences and concerns as they feel worthless)

- Withdraws Love (withhold our greatest quality from others but even more tragically from ourselves)

- Hurts as Hurt (often over reacts and lashes out from perceived attacks, mostly due to own insecurity)

--

At its highest, most conscious, loving and abundant (fluid and creative) form,

Feminine's positives are:

- Done to (Penetrated) (by the world and masculine)

- Seeks Connection (looks to build and maintain strong relationships)

- Receptive

- Open & Inviting (like a warm bath or ocean)

- Magnifies & Reflects (others' qualities back to them)

- Nurtures & Nests (creates warm home environment for themselves and their family)

- Forgiving (allows mistakes and limits judgment)

- Follows (open to be lead by a strong, clear, masculine energy)

- Senses (intuitive and feeling oriented)

- Security Seeking Creature (seeks financial, emotional and psychological safety/comfort)

- Trust is Everything (the feminine opens up ONLY when trust is created over time)

So as you can see, to Live It! as a fully integrated woman, you need to become the type of person that spends the majority of your time in the upper feminine. Whenever you are angry, depressed or frustrated, you are in the lower (fear) quadrant. It is key to add here, that as a woman you also have masculine strengths and weaknesses (left side of the diagram).

--

"It takes courage to grow up and become who you really are." [1]

~ **e.e. cummings**

---

1   http://www.quotegarden.com/be-self.html

Chapter 5

Men Living It!

"God has given you one face and you make yourself another." [1]

~ William Shakespeare

Men Living It!

Courageous Authenticity Real Life Story: **Cutting Off an Abusive Spouse and Mother**

"I acted courageously when I was living with a Borderline Personality Disorder (BPD) girlfriend (and mother of my child) and had to make the decision to break up with her and revoke her sponsorship in the country, and risk (permanently) losing contact with my 3 year old daughter. It was one of the toughest decisions of my life. But the alternative was to live in a hell, ruin my kid in the process, and ruin my own life as well.

There are times in life when as an authentic man, you have to step to the plate, strap your balls on, and do the right thing. But there are also moments like this that separate the winners from the losers in life, and define a man's true essence of who they are. I truly believe that what doesn't kill you makes you a much stronger, balanced, empathetic person. This was one of those times." Brian Y.

--

Never Had A Dad

As I grew up I became all too painfully aware that I didn't have a dad like (I thought) the other kids did. I believe the lack of a suitable father made living my life in courageous authenticity a challenge. I now know that many men have not had a dad either.

In kindergarten, I was constantly asked for my father's name and although I knew his name, he was not there. I felt shame as I thought it meant that I was unlovable. He had left my mom, fatherhood and the country when she was pregnant with me. By the time I was six years old, my mom had a new man in her life, but I still didn't have a dad, or what I thought was a father.

90

> ***My stepdad was a workaholic and when he***
> ***was home he was tired, angry, or distant.***
> ***Growing up for me was never safe.***

In my young mind, dads on TV were always portrayed as doing things with their sons like playing hockey or baseball; doing things that were fun. My stepdad was a workaholic and work Nazi. When he was home he was tired, angry or distant. He had two other kids from a previous marriage who he always had nice things to say about and more time for. The fact he was a travelling clothing entrepreneur meant he spent weeks at a time away on business. Those times when he was away were great as that was when I could spend time with my mom and not worry about his raging personality dysfunctions. The house was much more fun, loving and free then.

By the time I was eight, my stepfather had verbally and physically abused me as he was a frustrated bully (who knows if he was treated the same as a child). I knew what to do to stay out of his way and knew that if I did something my mom didn't like and she said *"I'll tell your stepdad"*, I knew I was going to get it, whatever blend of verbal or physical abuse "it" was. As an astrologist once told me, *"Growing up for you was never safe."*

Indeed it wasn't. I'm not alone. Many other men have had similar experiences with fathers who were either physically absent or worse, emotionally absent and abusive presences.

I Became A (Not So Nice) "Nice Guy"

I swore that when I grew up I would be different and not be abusive. What I didn't know was that becoming a "Nice Guy" had many pitfalls that were actually in many ways worse than the original abusive behavior that I despised. More on this will follow.

> *"Contrary to the prevailing sentiments of the last few decades, it is OK to be a guy."*
> *~ Dr. Robert Glover*

Cavemen Within Us

As men, we were born to Live It! All of our natural inborn and chromosomal characteristics and DNA push us constantly to powerfully take and create what we want out of life. For a man, to not be courageously authentic is almost worse (my male opinion here) than for women who are at least naturally less aggressive. Men shouldn't be passive. We are warriors and we are hunters (hunting down a big account is similar to hunting down a buffalo!). As discussed in Chapter 4, this doesn't mean that both men and women DON'T have a blend of masculine and feminine characteristics.

Don't let the fact that 100,000 years of time have passed since we lived as cave men and cave women confuse you. This period in evolutionary terms is a blink of an eye. All around our (supposedly) civilized societies it is clear to see that the caveman (and cave woman) lives. If these natural and primal tendencies are thwarted by laws and regulations, their unhealthy expression will explode in much more negative ways. From gangs, drugs, alcoholism and pornography (to name just a few) all can be easily explained by the fact strong masculine forces are still at work and must be expressed by men in some way. The expression is either healthy (career drive, passion, sports, adventure, sex) or unhealthy (rage, alcohol/sex/drug abuse, crime, gangs).

Having passions and outlets for our powerful male energy is critical for becoming a balanced and fulfilled, well-functioning and authentic modern man. These outlets can include but aren't limited to sports, hobbies, travel, business and any other activities we chose to participate in that challenge us as men in specifically masculine ways.

> *Women may NOT EVEN like you or your (VERY AUTHENTIC) ideas and actions, but they DO repect that you are yourself (as opposed to people-pleasing)!*

It Is Ok To Be A Guy

Men have not had a positive image for a long time. The media and women's groups have been quite powerful at making manhood an easy to attack affliction! *"No More Mr. Nice Guy"* [1] by Dr. Glover is a book that in my opinion should be required reading for all men and I make it mandatory for all my men's circle members and coaching clients:

"Contrary to the prevailing sentiments of the last few decades, it is OK to be a guy. Men born after World War II had the misfortune of growing up during the only era of recent western history in which it was not always a good thing to be male. This was primarily the result of two significant family and social changes in the post war era: 1) boys were disconnected from their fathers and other healthy male role models, and 2) boys were forced to seek approval from women and accept a female definition of what it meant to be male."

---

1   *No More Mr. Nice Guy, Copyright 2000, Robert Glover*

Nurses at war, and of paramount importance, school teachers (elementary and junior high school) were (and still are) mostly women.

"As a result of these two dynamics, many boys and men came to believe that they had to hide or eliminate any negative male traits (like those of their fathers or other "bad" men) and become what they believed women wanted them to be (so called "Nice Guys"). For many men, this life strategy seemed essential if they wanted to be loved, get their needs met, and have a smooth life…."

Become A Swiss Army Knife

The impossible objective of having a smooth life was covered previously. Life is many beautiful wonderful things, but smooth isn't realistic. A much better objective for you would be to become better at handling whatever life throws at you in all life areas. You are becoming a better person as you mature, stronger after every battle and adventure.

Think of being a MacGyver [1] in life, able to make do and create out of what's around to survive and thrive…like becoming a Swiss army knife.

"Many Nice Guys have difficulty connecting with men because of the limited positive male contact they experienced in childhood. Because these men did not have a positive bond with their father, they never learned the basic skills necessary to build meaningful relationships with men."

Other than the traditional roles of employee, rock star or jock, where do men have good, well-balanced male role models?

---

[1] *MacGyver was an excellent TV series in the mid-eighties. He is a resourceful agent with an encyclopedic knowledge of science, able to solve complex problems with everyday materials he finds at hand, along with his ever present duct tape and Swiss Army knife. http://en.wikipedia.org/wiki/MacGyver*

Another common trait among Nice Guys is the belief that they are *different from other men*. This is why men's circles are so important. They allow men to realize they are NOT different from other men and that what they go through, other men also go through and there is strength, solidarity and solace just in knowing you are not a "freak" or "recluse" due to your different feelings and outlooks.

This distorted thinking usually began in childhood when they tried to be different from their "bad" or unavailable father. In adulthood, Nice Guys often create a similar dynamic with men in general.

Nice Guys may convince themselves they are different from (better than) other men because they believe:

They aren't controlling.

They aren't angry and rageful.

They aren't violent.

They are attentive to a woman's needs.

They are good lovers.

They are good fathers."

As he mentions, most people recoil (at NOT being a Nice Guy. This included me before I really accepted my "Nice Guy" way of being and it's misguidedness. We incorrectly feel the opposite of being nice is being a jerk and who wants that? He correctly <u>clarifies that: the opposite of crazy is still crazy!</u> He explains the "integrated male" as a man with strong traditional qualities.

--

If we look at Appendix 4, the Masculine and Feminine diagram, we can see that the Masculine (where many modern "Nice Guy" men - including me in the past - spend too much of their time) at its most fearful, unconscious, rigid and deprived. This is where you as a man, have no real functional and sustainable power. All you have is some (limited) force.

Lower, Fearful, (Unconscious) Masculine:

- Controlling (via games or aggression and rage)

- Dominating (and domineering, uses anger and physical strength to bully)

- Rigid (inflexible to other ideas, "my way or the highway!")

- Aggressive (can be verbally and/or physically and/or sexually)

- Rageful (remember the Hulk?!)

- Abusive (verbally, emotionally, sexually, physically)

- Destructive (psychologically, verbally, physically, emotionally to others and self)

- Hurts Before Hurt (lashes out aggressively in a proactive attack due to rage and feeling insecure)

You can see that most of modern society's problems with gangs, drugs, alcoholism, prostitution and pornography are probably stemming from the destructive if unchanneled emotions above.

Higher Conscious Masculine: (abundant, fluid and creative)

- Does to the world (penetrates the world and the woman, invades, think Vikings!)

- Powerful: (physically, financially, psychologically, emotionally, not to be confused with force)

- Disciplined (keeps his word, does whatever it takes to succeed at what he loves)

- Focused (almost single-minded as a successful warrior would have to be to survive, think Yoda and Luke Skywalker)

- Provides and protects (think caveman protecting family from marauders/animals)

- Leads (takes charge and leads from internal power not from force!)

- Ascertains (evaluates, measures, makes plans, strategizes)

- Seeks Mastery & Freedom (freedom from slavery, the boss and the rat race, mastery of work, hobbies, master of himself and his thoughts, ideas and emotions)

- A Problem-solving Machine (loves to resolve problems physical, emotional and mental, loves to be challenged and always rises to the level needed and doesn't quit)

- Consistency is everything (how you do one thing is how you do everything!)

Live It! Activity #11: Which of the lower masculine traits do YOU go to when not at your best (when your STUMPS is running the show).

_____   _____

_____   _____

If you want to Live It! you will study the "Conscious list". Better yet, print it off and display it for a while and refer to it as I do when I don't like how I react or over react.

Men, the fact is that women love a man who is clear and strong and genuine even if they're not sure what the attraction is about! They may not even like you or your (VERY AUTHENTIC) ideas and actions, but DO NOT ever think they don't respect that you are yourself! That's why jerks can be quite successful with women. I've often wondered why in the past. Now I realize that at least they are themselves and honest about what they are and accept their masculine primary urges.

An authentic man like that is a man they can trust, and for a woman trust is what attracts them. Dr. Glover confirms that trust for a woman has the same physiological and psychological effect as a woman's naked breasts has for men! I know. Who knew? You do now, so become trustworthy and take all that life has to offer you!

--

"He who trims himself to suit everyone will soon whittle himself away." [1]

~ Raymond Hull

---

[1] http://www.quotegarden.com/be-self.html

Chapter 6

What Do I Take and Why?

"We are what we pretend to be, so we must be careful about what we pretend to be." [1]

~ Kurt Vonnegut

---

1   http://www.quotegarden.com/be-self.html

What Do I Take and Why?

Courageous Authenticity Real Life Story: My Best "Friend" Hitting on My Boyfriend

I had just moved to Toronto in 1999 and had a great job and a boyfriend in Montreal, a 5 hour drive away. I was dating a wonderful man who truly cared for me and even drove down to see me as a surprise for a weekend! A week or two later in Montreal I had dinner with him and my best girlfriend. We had a great time.

As I spoke to my boyfriend on the phone over the next week I found out that my girlfriend had called my boyfriend and asked him out on a date. He had said no and told her that he was happily dating me.

I was enraged, as I felt my best friend had become a traitor and had crossed a line that could never be undone. I was about to put an end to the relationship with the man for other reasons so this put me in a difficult situation. Did I accept what my girlfriend did as the man would no longer be in my life, or was the principle of her breaking my trust over arching?

I was upset for a few days trying to decide what to do next. I called my boyfriend and left him in the nicest way I could. I immediately called my girlfriend and told her that what she had done was beyond reprehensible and that she had destroyed my trust in her. That day I took a very difficult decision but I knew in my soul it was the right one. I never spoke to her again.

~ Felicia M.

Twins

As covered in detail in Chapter 3, all of us have a nasty (mostly) hidden mental program or voice which I have playfully named our Saboteur Trickster Most Pathetic Self in U, or STUMPS [1] for short. It plays small and pretends it is looking out for you or helping you by limiting you and telling you certain things are dangerous (don't change, don't leave any/all of your job, marriage, family, etc.). It steals your joy, questions, mocks and denigrates your brilliance and greatness.

Luckily we have its absolute opposite too (think good angel on one shoulder and bad angel/devil on other shoulder). Its opposite is your incredible "Most Brilliant Self"! This is the voice of your highest conscious self, the voice that had you do what was hard but ultimately right or most beneficial to you. I will reference both as needed.

> *Get clear and strong on WHAT you want and WHY you want it. The HOW you are going to get it and WHEN is NOT for you to worry about. That's your Universal Manager's job.*

You Want A Courageously Authentic Life

I will assume at this point of the book, if you are still here with me, (did you know 95% of books purchased never get read?), that the idea of living a life of courageous authenticity sounds and feels powerfully compelling to you. So here we are at the point where we need to begin finding out what we want to choose so we can have some clarity in terms of what the heck do we really want to TAKE? What is important to you and why?

So to properly live all the abundance that's available

---

1 *STUMPS: An acronym I created in "Cobra in the Closet", it stands for Saboteur Trickster Most Pathetic Self in U. It is that little negative voice inside you that always says you will fail, you're not (insert: smart, young, old, worthy, attractive, slim, etc.) _____ enough etc. It is like a mind virus that feeds on itself the more airtime or bandwidth you allocate to it. It is the agglomeration of all the nasty things people have ever said to you rolled into one convenient, tricky, fear-based lying thought process. Once you start noticing them, they lose power. STUMPS are a PART of you, like your toe, but THEY ARE NOT you! That's the key!*

Live It: Your Courageously Authentic Life

(remember the universe is unlimited in its abundance), YOU need to get clear and strong on WHAT you want and WHY you want it. The HOW you are going to get it and WHEN is NOT for you to worry about. You need to stop thinking about that as it usually pushes away the arrival. Your Universal Manager (I call mine Mike) will handle the HOW and WHEN. Isn't it great? That's two less things to worry about! This is because if YOU haven't received "it" or don't seem to be close to getting it (whatever "it" is that you want) you tend to go upstream (higher numbered negative emotions such as Pessimism, Doubt, Worry and Fear) and that feels bad and pushes your rendezvous away.

--

Hidden Train Tracks Influence Our Choices

One of the best ways to get clear about how and why we behave and think in certain ways is the concept of values. Here is a definition [1] of values:

Values: *"Important and enduring beliefs or ideals shared by the members of a culture about what is good or desirable and what is not. Values exert MAJOR influence on the behavior of an individual and serve as broad guidelines in ALL situations."*

--

1 www.businessdictionary.com

Values Are Deep

As you can see, values are very powerful and actually quite rarely discussed or identified and/or explained in the superficial popular media. If we look at culture in terms of an onion it would look something like the diagram below:

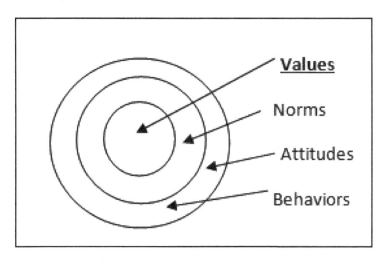

As you can see from the above diagram, what is seen/ heard by other people and ourselves are attitudes and behaviors. But Values influence our Norms, Attitudes and Behaviors - really, everything! It is very difficult (impossible?) to change a behavior without shifting our attitude. Our attitude changes by changing what we value.

Food For Comfort

In my earlier example about "getting disturbed" enough to lose weight, the original obese person obviously values food and eating MORE than health and energy or appearance. But we need to go deeper here. Why does this person love to eat? What do they get out of it? Well they get their need for certainty met. They know each meal will taste good, and they know they can eat and it will calm some of their fears or worries. They know they will get their need for variety met as every meal is different and can be exciting. They will get their need for significance met by eating at high end restaurants or cooking for others at home. They will get their need for connection by eating with others, or maybe from the staff of the restaurant.

Most eating disorders are emotional; since food provides comfort. Show me a person with weight issues and I see trauma and unresolved, unexplored emotional issues. All addictions work this way. I consider an addiction anything a person does to excess in a habitual and predictable way in times of stress. These can include, coffee, cigarettes, TV, shopping, alcohol, drugs (illicit and over-the-counter), sex and pornography, etc. We can even be addicted to being with other people! All are addicting and addictive.

It's the behavior that is the addiction and NOT just the habit.

> **Any goal or dream that doesn't align with your core values is dead, it can't happen, it is a fantasy.**

To shift themselves away from addictive excess food consumption, this person needs to begin cultivating a value of health and vibrancy that is higher than their need for comfort via food (safety, security, soothing). This is difficult to do, resulting in the obesity epidemic in many richer countries of the world. Food is particularly challenging as it is one of the only addictions where cutting the activity out completely is impossible. So this person needs to start equating health with connection and significance: get fit with friends or family, run a marathon, take pride in their appearance, attract and keep a partner.

Values Expanded

The following values paragraph and four exercises is a summary of the section of the values clarification exercise in the coaching book, Co-Active Coaching[1] . I've adapted it for our use here.

"Values are who we are, <u>not</u> who we would like to be, not who we think we should be, but who we ARE in our lives, right now! Values represent our unique and individual essence, our ultimate and MOST fulfilling form of expressing and relating. Our values serve as a compass pointing out what it means to be true to oneself. When we honor our values ON A REGULAR and consistent BASIS (by being courageously authentic), life is incredible and oh so fulfilling!

It is incredibly beneficial for you to get clear about your values. Critical life decisions are easier to make AND outcomes are more fulfilling when viewed through a matrix of well understood personal values. The process of clarifying is often difficult as our minds tend to fantasize when we really need to <u>look into the actions of our lives</u> to uncover the values that are already there, in our day-to-day actions and interactions.

Selecting values from a list DOESN'T work as it becomes a popularity contest for the most socially desirable values rather than a mechanism to see who you are. A list also intellectualizes the exercise and encourages "figuring it out" and "getting the words right." Your values live in the world. They are observable, <u>so picking from a list is useless.</u>

You can use values to know yourself, to make fulfilling choices, to strategize appropriate actions, and to recognize situations where values are an issue. Adding to the complexity is that you may have a completely different meaning for the same word for a value than the next person."

---

1   Whitworth, Kimsey-House (2), Sandahl, *Co-Active Coaching: New Skills for Coaching People Toward Success in Work and Life*, pages 245-248

Live It: Your Courageously Authentic Life

So let's find out what YOUR values are because then you will know those you can begin focusing on what YOU really want. <u>Any goal or dream that doesn't align with your core values is dead, it can't happen, it is a fantasy.</u> Determining YOUR values is critical for you to experience a fulfilling life.

--

<u>Values Clarification Exercise</u> [1]

Be aware it may take several months to complete this list, so don't rush!

> ***Since values emerge over time in our lives they are unlikely to occur at just one sitting.***

The first tip is to use a pencil with an eraser so you can make changes easily as it is NOT important to get them right the first time. The second tip is to use several words together to form a string. Separating them with a slash makes them easier to read.

<u>Examples:</u>

Integrity/Honesty/Walk-the-talk

Integrity/Whole/Congruent

Leadership/Empower/Collaborative

Leadership/Decisive/Powerful

Place the <u>most significant term at the beginning.</u>

Since values emerge over time in our lives **they are** unlikely

1   Whitworth, Kimsey-House (2) Sandahl, Co-Active Coaching: New Skills for Coaching People Toward Success in Work and Life, pages 245-248

to occur at just one sitting. A strong list of values is a powerful tool for you to refer to when it comes to fulfilling choices as you approach major crossroads or fall off track.

The following four scenarios will give you a place to start.

--

Value-Discovering Exercises

1. A Peak Moment in Time

Identify four special and critical moments in your life that were especially rewarding or poignant. It is important to use a very limited time frame to best identify values (a few hours or a day). Once you have a moment in mind answer the following.

What and when was the moment: _____

What was happening: _____

Who was present and what was going on: _____

What were the values being honored in that moment: _____

_____

What and when was the moment: _____

What was happening: _____

Who was present and what was going on: _____

What were the values being honored in that moment: _____

_____

What and when was the moment: _____

What was happening: _____

Who was present and what was going on: _____

What were the values being honored in that moment: _____

_____

What and when was the moment: _____

What was happening: _____

Who was present and what was going on: _____

What were the values being honored in that moment: _____

_____

--

2. Suppressed Values

Another way to dig to find or isolate values is to go to the exact opposite, looking at a time when you were angry, frustrated or upset. This will often lead to identifying a value that was being suppressed or ignored. Fill in the two examples below.

<u>Example 1:</u> **"I felt trapped, backed into a corner with no options."**

Values in example: value of freedom, choice or options

Your issue (stopping/running you):_____

Flip it over (Values) _____

Name the feelings and circumstances around the upset:

_____

The above is very effective as we get upset when something gets in the way of our honoring our values. We have usually set up our lives to honor our values (example, travel vs. family, security of pay cheque vs. excitement of small business). The bottom line here is that every time there is a moment of upset or distress it is always a value being suppressed.

--

3. **Must-Haves**

A third way to identify values is to look at what you MUST have in your life. Beyond the physical requirements of food, shelter and community, what must you have in your life in order to feel fulfilled? Must you have a form of creative self-expression? I do in my speaking, books and men's circles. Is having adventure and excitement in your life critical? I do with travel, motorcycling and other adventurous hobbies. What about partnership and collaboration? I do with my project partners and significant other. How aboutmoving towards a sense of accomplishment or success? Must you be surrounded by natural beauty?

A great question here is, *"What are the values you must have or a part of you dies?"*

--

Live-It! Activity #12: What are the values you absolutely must honour, or part of you dies? For me, if I can't honour my "freedom" value a big part of me dies.

_____   _____

_____   _____

--

4. **Obsessive Expression**

We are all capable of obsessive behavior, insisting on honoring a value, or inflating it into a demand rather than a form of self-expression. You've probably had an experience like this in your own life, such as when your roommate's value of orderliness became an obsessive demand for perfection. Your friends and families do you a great service by pointing out the obsessive expression of your values:

"You are SO controlling!"

"All you think about is your students."

"You want ALL the attention."

These statements probably point toward a value of personal power / leadership / learning / growth, and of recognition / acknowledgment.

--

Live It! Activity #13: Take a look at those times when you have taken certain values to the extreme. What is it that people said about you? What did you say about yourself? What is it that people teased you about or that drive them crazy? These are important values that have mutated for some reason (ego? fear?). Look for the value and don't focus on the mutation.

_____

_____

"Why try to be someone you're not? Life is hard enough without adding impersonation to the skills required." [1]

~ **Robert Brault**

1 http://www.robertbrault.com

Chapter 7

Vision Boards: Clarity Leads to Authenticity

"There's a 50% chance you won't like me... There's a 100% chance I won't change because of it!" [1]

~ Unknown

Vision Boards: Clarity Leads to Authenticity

Courageous Authenticity Real Life Story: **A Few Hoops?**

"As I approached these four figures - all but one who were acquaintances - I felt like something was out of place. Sporting my basketball gear, as I was on my way to shoot some hoops, I had agreed to sell a dego (1g of marijuana) to these individuals, shaking every ones' hand and introducing myself to the guy I wasn't yet acquainted with.

This guy I had just met decided to punk/rob me of my dego and tried to beat me up as well. He tried to instigate an evidently unfair fight, but I just laughed at his challenge as I weighed the value of my life/health against the insignificant dego.

The choice was obvious, I was not about to damage my body because of my pride. Before I walked away I asked them if they were down to go play some ball. Not to my surprise, they declined my offer, and so as I walked I knew they all had some deep insecurities and were certainly more concerned about their reputation."

~ Darko M.

--

Adults Have Dreamscapes On Their Walls

Do you remember when you were a teenager and you had all those posters and things up on the walls? Those things allowed you to dream fully and live in expectation of a wonderful future. How many posters of what you want in your life do you have now? If you are like 99.99% of people, you don't have ANY posters on your walls anymore. You chose at some point to not put them up as you were an adult and too cool or grown-up for it. Well, getting rid of visual dreams and things that inspire us is a lot of things, but cool is NOT one of them. We are visual creatures and we need to see what we want in our lives.

Enter The Vision (Dream) Board

One of the topics that I speak about that consistently elicits the most curiosity, questions and puzzlement, is the concept of vision (also called dream) boards. Most people I come in contact with just don't understand vision boards and who can blame them? Truth be told, I'm still NOT quite sure of HOW they work, but I can tell you THEY REALLY WORK AMAZINGLY WELL! Often touted as the "be all and end all" of manifestation, I prefer to see them as a key

cornerstone to harnessing (maximizing) the Law of Attraction. In this chapter, I will explain how I believe they can be created in the most enjoyable, simplest and most powerful way possible.

> *Being authentic requires that you know what you prefer and requires clarity. A vision board can provide that clarity.*

A vision board is a uniquely powerful vehicle which allows you to generate immediate movement towards significant improvements in your life. Constructing one is fun, creative and can harness the staggering power of four of your greatest helpers: 1) your intuition, 2) your integrity, 3) your subconscious mind, and 4) you are a visual being taking in over 60% of your sensory information through your eyes.

Now that you have connected to and created your values in Chapter 6, we can go to the next step: vision boarding. If you haven't completed your values, please GO BACK AND DO SO NOW or skip this chapter.

Clear Visions

It is time to create something visible that allows you to see your future dreams and imagine them as already happening! Being authentic requires that you know what you prefer. This requires clarity. A vision board provides that clarity. It focuses your energies and eyes on very positive and authentic-looking and photo-realistic wonderful things, people and experiences. These are the natural visible extension of your values. So a vision board is a visual representation of all you want.

I have real $100 bills on my vision wall right next to a picture of a money tree! Being clear on what you want means you have preferences. *With clear preferences it is easier for you to say yes and no to what you want.* Getting clear on what you are saying no to so you can say yes is very insightful and empowering (Empowerment: #1 on the ES).

--

Live It! Activity #14: Complete the following. "If I say YES to this, I am saying NO to this." Here's an example: "If I say YES to completing this book, I must say NO to watching late night TV."

1. "If I say YES to_____ I am saying No to _____.

2. "If I say YES to _____ I am saying No to _____.

3. "If I say YES to _____I am saying No to _____.

4. "If I say YES to _____ I am saying No to _____.

5. "If I say YES to _____I am saying No to _____.

Like attracts like.

Knowing what you are saying YES and NO to will allow more courageous authenticity, which is what you want! Of course 100% courageous authenticity is a chimera, as living in a society with laws and social structures requires some level of adaptive social tact to survive and fit in. I believe the level of your authenticity is on par with your level of clarity (of who you are, what you want and why you want it). The vision board activity is fun and provides a very high level of clarity.

My First Vision Board

On my vision board above, you can clearly see my values laid out with motivating pictures and environments that speak to me. These are beautiful to me and inspire me. I will outline my vision board's thoughts and feelings process a little further, not because it is right, but simply to use as an example of how I put it together. My subconscious mind processes these images into my brain and I begin to feel as if I already have those things, and act like I have them ALREADY. This in turn attracts those things into my life. Remember, *like attracts like.*"

I took it one step further (actually seven steps further) by creating a vision wall. A combination of eight vision boards (4' wide x 2' tall) connected to make a full supercharged manifesting wall. This has allowed me to exponentially accelerate the "attraction power" of this fun and potent visual tool.

I will explain how:

a) I got involved,

b) Why I believe they work,

c) How to create your own,

d) What should be included and what other life adjustments need to be made to maximize your speed and size of manifestation from leveraging and believing in this amazing tool.

--

Vision Board Genesis

Why would you want to create a vision board? A vision board will fast forward the achievement of all the dreams you place on it! It will allow you to be clear and authentic in terms of what you want in your life. Here's how I got started.

In 2006 I watched and had my eyes opened by the movie *"The Secret."* [1] This documentary first introduced me to the Law of Attraction which I have endeavored to practice extensively since to the best of my best abilities. The story of a man who had created a vision board which had a huge mansion on it particularly captured my interest. He found the vision board years later as it was packed

---

1   *Secret, Movie, www.thesecret.tv*

in moving boxes. His son was rummaging around and found the long forgotten and dog-eared board. After looking closely at a mansion he had placed at the center of the board, he was awestruck as he realized he was living in the house that was ON THE vision board!

He hadn't noticed it was the same mansion, as the picture of the house he had just bought and moved into (on his vision board) had been taken as an aerial photograph. His subconscious had probably taken that image of the house and helped him choose it years later without his conscious awareness. This blew me away. How was that even possible? The odds were simply too staggering to entertain.

> *How could he have moved into the house that was on the vision board without some grand(divine?) design (Universal Manager?)?*

Let's dig deeper. He put a picture of a dream home on his vision board and within ten years he had bought it and lived there. He had NOT actively tried to search out the house. Even if he was focused on getting that house and had tried, he would have had to sell his prior house at exactly the same time that this new house was on the market! The fact he had bought it without knowing suggests powerful (unseen, but like electricity and gravity, very real) forces were at work. Firstly in his subconscious mind, secondly in his intuition, and thirdly with the help of his "Universal Manager" who orchestrated this perfect, complex symphony. Anyone with even a very basic understanding of probability and statistics would agree that this was a one in a billion/trillion chance, and yet it happened.

--

A Client Gets Me Into Vision Boarding

In 2011, I was working closely with a coaching client. I was trying to bring clarity, perspective and purpose to the meaning of her life. I watched *"The Secret"* and the vision board jumped out at me again.

The next day, I purchased the necessary materials for my client and I to both create vision boards. I was very excited when I coached her and wanted the creation of the vision boards to be fun. The vision board seemed like a blast and I wanted to manifest with one too! The reasons I wanted one were: a) to support my client, b) to be clearer on my purpose and direction as well, c) they are totally visual and I am very visual, d) I'm a dreamer at heart!

So we began our vision boards in parallel!

--

Vision Board Materials

Step: 1 Values Clarification

We purchased cork boards, push pins, and magazines containing our interests. I purchased a men's outdoor magazine and another high-end home magazine and my client purchased a woman's magazine and a nature magazine. We also had some business newspapers, the ones with nice, glossy colour paper.

The first step in vision board creation is to determine your own values, which we did in the last chapter.

Vision Board Examples

Before I explain how I created mine, I thought I would share some vision board examples with you with my comments.

What I love about this vision board (above) is the international feel and grandiose scale of the pictures and environments. The clearly defined values (romance, adventure, friends, family, travel, success, etc.) are also represented by specific clusters of images. The positive mantras and words obviously connect to the creator. This is a brilliant example of a vision board that really excites and motivates, which is exactly what a vision board should do!

This above is also an excellent example of what works. Here the images are separated by space giving an "ocean" or "sky" vastness that really works. The money hedge is an iconic piece that sets the stage for an adventurous and luxurious feel augmented by the picture of the airplane. The very observant among you will quickly notice that the elements are well balanced, with sky, water, fire and earth pictures. The one downside to this one is that clear values have not been affixed, losing some of the subconscious power that a proper, value-listed vision board can create. Nevertheless, it's a great vision board.

This board is a great example of someone with an unquenchable passion for extreme sports, adventure and action! The sheer movement and adrenaline of this board motivates its creator to action. The addition of motivational phrases such as *"Go Big"*, *"Destined for Glory"*, *"Give up Nothing"* and *"Win Big"* show an ambition, fearlessness and renegade spirit that is contagious!

Ironically, six months after this board was created, its owner had an incredible brush with death! As he was doing what he loved, back country mountain biking, he had a bad crash. He severed one of his fingers right off. He tore a piece of his jersey, wrapped it around the digit, put it in his backpack and wrapped his remaining gushing finger stump. He then cycled two hours out of the back country feeling dizzy and ready to pass out at any moment from the shock.

He continuously told himself, *"This is not my last ride!"* He miraculously made it to his car and drove to the hospital where they successfully reattached his severed finger. He made a full recovery with the use of the finger as well. I believe that his authentic adventurous spirit created the initial incident but that same spirit saved him.

This one shows tremendously well organized themes and values and has good clusters. I would put the person's picture at the center though. The reason to put our picture in the center is to be crystal clear in our signal to the Universe that this is OUR board and this is OUR life and dreams!

This one has a clearly defined sensuality and feminine strength (the background was pink) with a sense of style and humour. The glitter glue around the edges adds to the artistic flair. As a piece of art, anything and everything can be placed on your vision board. For example, I have a bag of ashes from a fire walk I did at a Tony Robbins weekend. To me, it means doing the impossible as I severely burned my feet as a young child. Go crazy! If it means something to you, it MUST go up on the board!

This vision board is one of my favorites. The honesty of the board and the sky blue background really open it up. The pictures are very, very high-end and show a level of desire for luxury far above the norm, and as such have that much more attraction and manifesting power! The majestic horse represents royalty/nobility, grace and freedom. The endless pool represents luxury as does the yacht, super barbeque, luxury sports cars, watch and home. It's a very powerful board indeed.

This one is great in its details and cool words and sayings. It's dynamic, active and fun to discover; a real treat.

Although I would not generally suggest black as a background colour, this board pulls it off. This one has a classy, jazzy buttoned-down feel to it.

Hopefully these examples have excited you with the possibilities!

Step 2: Picture Selection

This next step is so much fun. I invite you to do it with your partner or friends and have a vision board party! Get yourself into a happy, expectant and positive frame of mind. Perhaps you could enjoy a drink to celebrate the fact you are about to embark on a magical journey that will allow you to visualize and attract abundance into your life!

Go out and buy magazines. Go through your magazines and just look at the pictures and see what feelings emerge. When one grabs your attention, fold that page, mark it with a post-it note, or rip it out. In my experience, I find you need to look at pictures at LEAST two or three times to really get drawn in. This will also allow you to see if you experience a permanent connection to the image or just what I call the "eye candy" effect. This effect is when a picture catches your attention but there really is no deep desire or passion for what the picture suggests. This explains why during the second review you really start to find the perfect pictures for you. Tip: allow your eyes to meander over the picture and your mind to visit the experience that the picture suggests. Hopefully, you will be able to find at least 30 to 50 good pictures.

> *A vision board/wall should NEVER resemble ordinary or everyday life.*

By now you should be having a lot of fun! Imagining exotic destinations, experiences, relationships and achievements that take you away and enchant you! Daydream again like when you were a kid! Ensure the pictures are really of exciting, opulent or dynamic things. *A vision board/wall should NEVER resemble ordinary or everyday life.* You don't need vision for that. If your pictures do look ordinary, take a break and do it another time when your passion and creativity are at the ready. The vision board should pull you powerfully into your life in an exciting and dynamic display of colours, motion, scenery and magic! The objective is to convey powerful emotions.

Step 3: Mounting Your Pictures

A cork board and pins will allow flexibility, which at first will definitely be needed as you place pictures all over the board. I found that at first I put them all up to see them. Then I started moving them around into clusters that looked like the pictures belonged together. I will use my first vision board (one of the nine boards I currently have as a vision wall) as an example for you.

> *We tend to believe what is written in large, fancy, important looking letters, whether true or not. Than a lifetime of Pavlovian training by mass advertising.*

You will also need many newspapers as you will be cutting the largest letters to write your own quotes or sayings. This utilizes the negative power of the media in a positive way for you. We tend to believe what is written in large fancy letters, whether true or not. By doing this, we can program ourselves with the right words on our boards.

--

Frank's In-Depth First Vision Board

I believe my insights will help give you ideas and tools to create a more powerful vision board for yourself. If you can avoid the mistakes I made, then that's a positive factor! Although, we do learn from all our mistakes.

I started with my first board and moved things around a few times before I glued them in final positions. Amazingly, I am still (18 months later) very happy with how it flows and feels to me. When you get it right, it stays right.

129

Live It: Your Courageously Authentic Life

Let's begin with my first board.

Let's begin at the top left of my first board. Values of Nature and Adventure are clearly exemplified by a skier exploring mountains and a beach. The vintage motorcycle represents freedom to me and the brand or type is irrelevant (I ride an adventure bike and this is a custom). The image's idea is what is important, not its detail.

Over to the middle top we see values of Success/ Achievement. Here you will find my obsession with high-end watches (I own a TAG Heuer but want them all!) is apparent. To me these are the only jewelry I wear and I love them. They represent being a successful gentleman with class, practicality, adventure and grace!

> *A Greek island home overlooking the ocean with servants at my beck and call, feels rich and successful and wonderful!*

Below, my value of Passion is characterized with a couple (romantic passion), driving a car (freedom and movement) and the open road signifying life's adventure. It also reminds me that we can only handle 200 feet of road right in front of us at a time at night. Yet, we still can cross the country. to focus on the here and now and not worry about what might come (fear, loss) later. This is a primary reason why Live It!'s cover depicts a car driving on a sinewy mountain road by the ocean.

At the top right we see my value of Creativity with a book and a castle exploding from it. Given that I fancy myself a creator of self-help and children's books, this picture still powerfully motivates me.

At the top right is my value of Luxury/Comfort represented by a Greek island home overlooking the ocean with servants at my beck and call. It FEELS rich and successful and wonderful! Looking down and towards the center, a super elite class seat in a plane and a fireplace add to the luxury/comfort vibe. The walk-in closet also exemplifies the look and feeling of opulent living. Vision boards are powerful as they capture the feeling of a goal and the goal / achievement / situation and help it come to life!

Back at the nine o'clock position, we see a diver going to a plane wreck which represents pure adventure and excitement. I don't even dive, but it is the representation of it that takes me away!

Below that is another nod to a Luxury/Comfort vibe with cigars and high end liquor. The fact that I don't smoke or drink much is secondary here as well, as these represent "having made it" to me. A home with these things in it is a great home indeed, warm and inviting! Also it underscores a value of "Connection" as you don't usually drink or smoke cigars alone.

> *Men around a campfire represent masculine connection which has manifested forme over the last year.*

Next, at the center we can see MMA fighter Georges St. Pierre (GSP) who represents the top of his industry, mixed martial arts. He is champion at 170 lbs welterweight, I weigh 175 lbs. Additionally, he is from my home town of Montreal. More importantly, he represents Health and Fitness and someone in full vibrant health. Below him is a picture of a comfortable, distinguished and healthy looking, older Richard Gere. This represents aging gracefully and still being attractive and warm.

Below that, you can see two race/sports type of cars which are another one of my passions. As a "gearhead", I love any/ everything that goes really fast and vibrates and wails like a banshee. When I become much more financially wealthy (note the language of positive expectation and belief, both are #4 on the ES), I want to race cars and own super fast sports cars, motorcycles and planes.

At the bottom right, we see a group of men around a campfire and that represents masculine Connection. This has manifested for me over the last year with my men's circles and other male friendships. Pictures of dogs add to comfort and connection values for me. The gorilla is powerful, wild and cool! Randomness also works well in a vision board.

The bottom right is filled with pictures of adventure-type travel I endeavour to experience. Examples include flying a jet, riding dirt bikes in Baha, Fiji etc.

Big goals are easier. Religions don't have a monopoly on faith.

My Second Board

Within days I had other images I wanted to capture and so I began a second vision board which was directly above the first one. I figured since I was so visual more pictures of everything I wanted for myself would be better. I say, "GO BIG OR GO HOME!" Once you commit to something, in this case (a vision wall) a whole slew of events co-conspire to make magical things occur.

I guess that would be the genesis of what became my vision wall, which currently takes up a whole wall of my living room!

For the second board, a great alter ego emerged and that was the idea of my being a *"Super Jedi Coach"*. As ludicrous as it may seem, I was listening to John Kehoe and realized that if I could embrace that term, I would become it! It captured my imagination and connected to my heart and soul. I also added more high-end watches, including a Rolex and two others, some money, Porsches, a great cottage view, more money, a beautiful travelling case, a beautiful woman and a vehicle. Two powerful phrases are on this board, *"Big Goals are Easier"* (because they have vision and purpose), and *"Religions Don't Have a Monopoly on Faith."* Faith is # 4 on the ES (Positive Expectation and Belief) and where most religions access their flock. This second board proved to me that additional boards were possible and actually preferable!

Persevere even when your exterior circumstances show no results, and ESPECIALLY when you're NOT getting results.

--

Third Board

    This above is board #3. Here I began writing very powerful maxims and sayings in creative and important looking letters, many from John Kehoe[1]. I now believe all of these, not just in my mind (intellectual understanding) but at a much deeper (cellular) level. Belief/Faith is #4 on ES. This stems from my focus on training with his principles.

"Your wealth can make a difference."

    This sentence helped me so much because it addressed a long held limiting belief. I used to believe that when someone became wealthy, they took that wealth from someone else. This is false as the universe is limitless and abundant (as covered in detail in Chapter 2). Remember, one person's wealth can help many people.

---

1   Kehoe, John, "Mind Power for the 21st Century, Zoetic Books

Just think of all the people who make money when you are on vacation: the airlines, rental car companies, hotels, restaurants, all small shops or activities, etc.

--

"The power in you is greater than the outer reality."

~ John Kehoe

This one helped me realize that my power is unlimited and unrelated to what is happening outside me, and that we create our own destiny despite external circumstances and conditions. As Kehoe says, *"Persevere even when your exterior circumstances show no results, ESPECIALLY when you're NOT getting results."*

--

"Superdog: #1 NY Times Best Seller List"

This one began pre-accepting the success of my children's book project.

--

"This is not a practice life!"

This one is SOOOO big, I have it as the signature on my email, at the closure of every weekly newsletter as my salute at the back of the book. To me it says, we don't get a redo, we get one pass at every moment. It is our duty to live our most authentic life full out.

--

Live It: Your Courageously Authentic Life

> *"I will lead, not follow! Step up!"*

> ~ Tony Robbins

This one allows me to tap into my leadership power, which I always thought of as weak or diffuse. I realized that I am more of a Richard Branson (fun, adventurous, loving) leader than a cold distant autocratic one. But I am definitely a leader now.

--

> *"Be BOLD, be Courageous."*

This one pushed me to try different and unconventional approaches. The trying of different things allowed me to fail (not succeed). The failing made me learn and then try again a little differently and ultimately I succeed much more permanently each time.

Try new thing→Failure→ Learning→ Try again→ Growth→ Success→ Try new thing

--

I added one that's not in the picture:

> *"Stay hungry, stay foolish!"*

> ~ Steve Jobs

These are such tremendously powerful maxims, that by reading them daily, I program and command subconscious mind so it can create the conditions for attaining what I see. I wrote myself a check for $100,000 for a book/movie advance. That didn't happen, so I removed the date. That stopped the pressure and I became focused again, instead of thinking, *"Why isn't it happening?"* (Doubt, #13 on

136

the ES) I was disconnected and attracting more discussion. I stayed in doubt for a few weeks, but I had suffered enough and continued to work hard because I loved what I was creating.

You can also see the real money bills that feel like they're manifesting for me nicely. So I suggest real money (money is a vibration and energy, so you want real money pulling in real money).

> ### *Take life (the tiger) by the tail*
> ### *"A lion never makes excuses for what he is."*

--

Fourth Board

Here, if we begin at the top left, is a clock (signifying organization and focus) and a tiger. I love tigers as they are beautiful, regal and powerful! They only kill for food or self-defence, and to me this signifies Power and not Force. I want to take life (the tiger) by the tail!

Then there is a staircase with gold running down signifies opulence. There's a picture of Oprah as I want to see/hear myself interviewed by her (I imagine it often!) or have a show on her network because once you are on her show, everything launches at a huge exponential level and I can help more people.

Next, there is a racing motorcycle (no explanation required, I love bikes!), then a luxurious, attractive woman in an opulent place. More watches! A fast sports car and license plate and palm tree from where I want to live: Los Angeles. On the left we see a sand bar with houses on it, a lift ticket to Mammoth Mountain in California, Porsches on the beach in Malibu and a luxury Bentley. Phrases include: "In the moment" (a reminder to stay present), and "Definitely Winning" (Charlie Sheen). There is also a great maxim from Kehoe:

Will (decision) + Imagination + Action = Massive Results

--

Next, is a tuxedoed picture of me to remind me of being at a high-end event on a Hollywood red carpet; my logo: "2BFRANK". I am really proud of that creation (thanks Pete W!) and representation of what my (personal) brand is and means →complete authenticity!

The final piece here is my Life Purpose Statement (In Chapter 7 you will get to create yours!).

"I am the unstoppably fearless lion that demonstrates courage to dramatically wake people up to their Most Brilliant Selves."

Creating that bold metaphor produced a huge shift for me as it allows and actually encourages me to act like a lion in the service of my coaching clients, readers, 2BFRANK Men's Circles [1] and audiences. The lion is courageous, regal, proud and the *"King of the Jungle"*. Another related quote is *"A lion never makes excuses for what he is."* How's that for courageous authenticity?

> ***That illustration kept the dream alive for me over the difficult eighteen months I've been imagining and wishing.***

--

Fifth Board

This became the planning board that allowed me to see all my projects and create the timelines for each. It is like a military strategy board to help me with my usual creative genius laced with disorganization. Amazingly most of the projects I put there and focused on consistently are happening or well on their way! This is why it works: *"What you focus on, grows"*. I focused on this a lot!

At the top you can see the letters for "Masks Off!" which is a game I created to deeply and authentically connect people. Then we can see more great maxims across the board:

"Opportunities are everywhere!"

"My subconscious mind is my partner in success." (Kehoe)

"I have unlimited power at my disposal." (Kehoe)

"Frank the super salesman sells the sizzle!"

"My imagination and power of thought can create everything I want!"

Half obscured: *"My success helps many people, my failure helps no one."*

--

Live It! Activity #15: Compare the above maxims to the messages you have around you. Perhaps that is why YOUR mind isn't visualizing great things and messages? Begin questioning all messages coming into you and only seeking positive meanings.

--

Next we can see three columns with my major projects, all of which have materialized, plus the "inner circle." My men's circles are currently called *"2BFRANK Men's Circles"*; close enough! You can see at the top right a coloured drawing of my kids' Superhero dog story. I can't tell you how much appreciation and joy (both are #1 on the ES) that one gave and still gives me as I am putting final touches on the story with my illustrator partner. That colour illustration kept the dream alive for me over the difficult eighteen months I've been waiting and wishing. I have tears of faith (#4 on the ES) now!

--

Sixth Board

This board has many interesting elements. Firstly, the hand with fingers holding buildings and airports signifies ownership of real estate and many businesses (which I want). To the right is a diagram explaining suffering and how we can't control things outside of us (Examples: boss, partner, economy, weather, etc., anything but ourselves). My watch obsession continues! Then, a brilliant picture which basically is as follows:

--

People Who Are Wrong

X X X X X X X X X X X X X X X

X X X X X X X X X X X X X X X

"x" = Lots

This encapsulates my thoughts! The media and many are disconnected from their values and authenticity. Taking direction or guidance from them is a classic case of the blind leading the blind. I also created a maxim called, *"I am a multitasking powerhouse and limitless."* The W.H. Murray quote below is very powerful and has reinforced my belief in the Law of Attraction. It is also from John Kehoe's *"Mind Power for the 21st Century"*:

"The moment one definitely commits oneself then providence moves too. All sorts of things occur to help one that would otherwise never have occurred. A whole stream of events issue from that decision, raising in one's favor all manner of incidents, meetings and material assistance which no man would have believed would have come his way."

~ W.H. Murray

--

Additionally, I included a few illustrations for my kid's superhero story and the brand plan I created with my cousin for said story. Below that, I have my Life Purpose Statement, covered in extensive detail in the next chapter. There is also a list of Kehoe's "6 Laws" as which we will cover in detail in Chapter 8.

--

Seventh Board

This board has a very pronounced freedom, nature and adventure vibe. From the top left:

"Leave ordinary at the station." A strong vote for my being a *"Zebra among horses"*.

"I bring 2.0 Brain Software to the world." Helping myself understand my role in the world and what I want to create.

"Think local, grow global." Realizing, L.A. will come in due time.

"Build it & they will come." Faith that whatever I create will thrive.

"Supply follows demand." The more we desire from the universe the more it gives.

"Frank's duty to the world: educate, help, coach and entertain." A huge mantra which every major project or event is tested by.

--

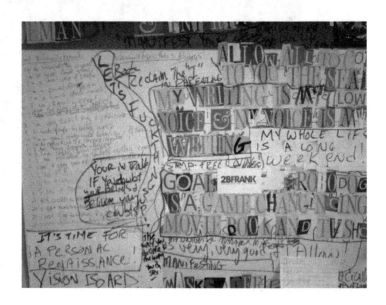

Eighth Board

In many ways this last board feels to me like it might be the one that has given me the most powerful support of them all.

At the top left is an exercise that I did (from John Kehoe), in which I created a list of twenty self-acknowledgments, the idea being to create a list of things I know to be true about myself. I suggest doing this when you are in good spirits, as otherwise they will be weak. Juicy language is important here! Self-acknowledgements are covered in more detail in Chapter 14. Some of the key mantras from this board include:

"Allow all to come to you. The sea is low, all rivers flow." from Wayne Dyer, meaning to "BE" is much more important than anything you "DO".

"My writing is my voice, my voice is my writing." This helped me to truly identify with myself as a writer vs. someone who writes. It also allowed me to step into sharing my passion through writing.

"My whole life is a long weekend!" In the past, I would complain on days that I "had" to go to teach. When I realized I had so much more free time than most, it helped me to appreciate this much more "free and open", abundant perspective.

"You're in trouble if you doubt your beliefs and believe your doubts." This very powerful quote is from Tony Robbins and it reminds me to believe and have faith (Positive Expectation, Belief are #4 on the ES).

"Goal: Superdog is a game-changing movie, book and TV show." This maxim has been my guide for the journey, is progressing well and should soon be available to the public. Some issues out of my control occurred and delayed the project, but I persisted and it's happening.

So that's my vision wall!

--

Live It! Exercise #16: Hopefully you are ready to create your future with a vision board!

--

In summary, creating vision boards will help you immensely to supercharge your feelings and visualizations which will accelerate your attraction pattern. By focusing, feeling and visualizing what you want, you send a crystal clear request to the Universe. It will reply to your request with full abundance when you allow (by staying in highest vibrations) it to. Although no one knows when, what you desire will come to you. The how and when it will happen is not your responsibility anyway.

--

"Because the truth is, it doesn't really matter who I used to be. It's all about who I've become." [1]

Unknown author

Chapter 8

Authenticity When We Are "Down"

"Most people are other people. Their thoughts are someone else's opinions, their lives a mimicry, their passions a quotation." [1]

– Oscar Wilde, De Profundis, 1905

---

1   http://www.quotegarden.com/Be-Self.html

Authenticity When We Are "Down"

Courageous Authenticity Real Life Story: I Lost Everything and I'm Fine

"And just like that, everything that was good that I had was gone in a flash: girlfriend, job, confidence and happiness. The things I took for granted I lost all at once and it took me by surprise, even though my attitude at the time should have alerted me to this event earlier. I was left directionless and feeling like there was nowhere to go. It's hard to pinpoint just because I can't really remember the one thing that helped me find my way.

I guess if I had to choose it would be me realizing that after talking to people that had been where I was before and coming to terms with the fact that it wasn't the end of the line for me, I just needed to look inside to find what I wanted people to think of me. This allowed me to pick myself up and clear away all the negative thoughts and start acting with a purpose. It was then that I finally found what I had always needed to keep moving forward. I found a goal and a reason to live."

~ Michael V.

--

Down Authentically and/or Authentically Down

On my best days I am convinced I have been given a very magical gift(s). These gifts include a range of abilities from intuition, empathy, openness, vision, intelligence, creativity, writing, etc. On my worst days I feel that my magical gift is actually a curse. I feel all my emotions very deeply and that can be difficult. This chapter aims to investigate courageous authenticity in those "not-so-great" days that we all have.

148

> **Putting a smiley face on your "gas gauge" of life**
> **doesn't fill up your tank!**

A book on courageous authenticity would be a farce and not very authentic if it did not breach the subject of how it looks or feels <u>when we are NOT</u> in the upper emotions. Authenticity is especially relevant in those states. I know this as I have been in a low mood for the last few days, almost like Charlie Brown walking around with a dark cloud over my head. I would estimate the feeling "down" as being from #16, Discouragement all the way to #22, Fear, Grief, Depression, Despair, and Powerlessness. How nasty that feels!

Authenticity in writing this book begins with me admitting that I have been feeling very down. The genesis of my mood is probably very similar to how it happens for you. A few events have occurred in my life that have me questioning my abilities, what I am creating and even who I am being. They have also taken me to an un-resourceful place where I attracted similar thoughts, circumstances and events. One thing that I am very aware of is the poor job I've done of framing what I am thinking/doing when I'm down. Framing is the attribution of meaning to events that occur.

In retrospect, I began attributing events that occurred as very negative, from people not returning my calls or cancelling previous engagements, to other people close to me moving ahead in their lives and acquiring luxury goods (ego). I began doubting, over thinking and micromanaging things instead of going with the flow and enjoying life and living in the present.

When we are down (for lack of a better emotional descriptor), it is imperative that we DON'T do what many people do, which is to mask or numb what we are feeling.

Putting a smiley face on your "gas gauge" of life doesn't fill up your tank!

Actually, it makes you feel worse because you are lying and not being authentic. Our ego, when we are in that place, tells us NOT to show weakness. Our egos argue that to show weakness will lead to others judging and ultimately rejecting and abandoning us (one of our greatest fears from childhood as it equates to death for an infant).

As adults we often act inauthentically for self-protection so that we won't be judged or perceived as too different. Everyone wants to be somewhat different, but there is resistance the further one moves from "common and societally acceptable" behaviour.

--

Our Lying STUMPS

The human mind is constantly working <u>like a machine without an "OFF" switch</u>. It thinks thoughts all the time, worried thoughts, hopeful thoughts, fearful, angry, passionate, exciting thoughts. Our STUMPS likes to play with us the same way a cat does with a half-dead mouse. All the intimate things it knows about our faults or limitations, it can and does use. Whatever it knows, it will project worst-case scenarios.

> *Negative thoughts attract experiences that confirm these negative thoughts.*

Our minds lie to us constantly as they tell us lies about things that never happen! You see, your mind knows all the hidden, worst aspects of who it thinks you are. As Kehoe advises, we cannot even trust the thoughts our mind thinks! In the absence of self-guidance, our minds are influenced (seeded) by our environment. Our environment is very negative. Our minds are great tricksters (what I call STUMPS) and can have us running on half-baked (negative) ideas and self-questioning thoughts based on half truths and plain lies.

Anxieties, worries, and fears are all useless thoughts. Fears we have around trying new things, approaching new people or fear of the future can't be dealt with when we are in such a non-resourceful place. They become catastrophizing and attract other similar negative thoughts. ***Those thoughts attract experiences that confirm these negative thoughts.*** Then the vicious negative cycle is created and reinforced.

When we are down, our STUMPS projects multiple worst-case scenarios and never even thinks twice about calling them "certainty" or "fact" when really they are but one opinion (aiming to keep us small), and certainly coming from the lower (scarcity) vibrations. Notice, that they never come with a disclaimer such as, *"this may or may not occur."* They very powerfully lie to you but do it convincingly with just the amount of truth to make it believable. They are just as smart as YOU are.

--

In this particular scenario for me, authenticity manifested itself in uttering my truth and lashing out at a business associate whose feedback on a new project I felt was very negative and unconstructive. It also showed up as calling a coach friend and literally crying it out as she suggested I take a break from working, to reconnect with myself and explore nature and be more playful.

These were all great suggestions and I am putting them to work. My wonderful girlfriend advised me to take good care and be gentle with myself. Additionally, she suggested that perhaps I had lost my balance, and forgot to remain present. I had run myself dry, which makes total sense. I do tend to be very hard on myself.

--

Live It! Activity #17: What do you do to take care of yourself when you are down? How are you gentle with your "baby soul"? One author [1] called his soul this after the tragic loss of his daughter and then wife in the same year.

--

In my case, being authentic with you here and now is about admitting my fear of going back to that dark and depressed state I was in about five years ago when I went through a very dark night. This fear comes up for me every once in a while, as my STUMPS grabs at whatever worst point of reference it can relate to. In this case that episode that obviously left a scar on my psyche healed, but has never fully disappeared.

> **_Your STUMPS is a nasty aspect of you and will never stop._**
> **_Your job is to realize that is a part of you_**
> **_but IS NOT all of who you are._**

The STUMPS Is A Part Of Us, But It Is NOT Us

The rational mind can only do so much when the STUMPS highjacks it and we give fear the reins of our life. The STUMPS very carefully and craftily focus on some truths about that episode but neglect to frame it with all the positives that came from that period.

---

1   Pearl, Neal, "Ghost Rider"

Specifically, for me those included becoming a coach, learning to help other people, and allowing me full access to those emotions in my work.

Yes, the STUMPS is a nasty aspect of us and will never stop doing what it does best. Our job is to realize <u>that is a part of us but IS NOT all of who we are.</u> **It is like your foot is part of you but is definitely not all of YOU.** These difficult times are periods in our lives when it's time to see what/who we truly are. It is easier to be authentic when you feel great and all external conditions are pleasing. However, I believe the <u>real work</u> is in remaining authentic NO matter the weather and geography of our moods or circumstances.

--

Life As A Roller Coaster

Our downs or lows also allow us to enjoy the highs of our lives. A great metaphor is a roller coaster. I have come to believe that our lives are like roller coasters and without the lows the highs are meaningless, as they are without contrast or comparison. Additionally there is quality and depth to the darkness.

I believe that it is in embracing <u>ALL</u> of who we are, ESPECIALLY the darker parts that we come alive and live a richer life. The lessons of the darker parts always become clearer when time has passed. We must trust (Faith #4 on the ES) that it is all part of our journey and learning in this life. A belief that the universe is benevolent and abundant helps tremendously to feel the fear and do it anyway, as Susan Jeffers [1] relates.

> *Fear is a strong signal and usually suggests we need to get more prepared (take action).*

---

[1] *Jeffers, Susan, Feel the Fear and Do it Anyway*

Fears Are Always Worse Than Reality

Most people mistakenly think that people who are successful are fearless. This is incorrect. They are fearful but put their hopes and dreams above/over their fears. Fear can be seen as an acronym.

F alse

E xpectations

A ppearing

R eal

So most of the things/events we do fear NEVER end up happening, and the less we fear things the less fearful things are attracted into our experience. Don't misunderstand me here, <u>fear is a very strong signal and usually suggests we need to be more prepared by taking action.</u> Fear is a good thing to keep us alive, but most modern fears are mind-created, and those are the ones to investigate, question and reframe. So don't just ignore fears, instead try to see if they are truly founded or STUMPS-induced (the worst case scenario all the time).

If we listen to the fear message and use it to be more prepared, that alleviates some of its power. As you get better at stepping through fear and acting anyway, you realize that 99% of the time the fear was MUCH worse than the reality. 1% of the time you were right; if you aren't paralyzed by fear you can deal with whatever the occurrence is in the moment much more effectively, as you have your wits about you.

An example for me is that I currently fear rejection by people when I ask them to join my men's circles. The longer I wait to meet people and ask, the more certain I am that no one will join and then the fear becomes greater and more entrenched. So as soon as my brochure is ready, I have committed to going to meet people in my community to let them know what I am doing. I probably need 11 no's for every yes. If I look at every no as 1/12 of yes, then I can do it (sales 101!).

In my experience with clients I have found that once we identify the fears that are manipulating us, they have MUCH LESS power over us. Taking action to reduce the fear is definitely important to get it under control, so that it (via the STUMPS) doesn't control us.

--

Live It! Exercise #18: Take a moment and list your current worst fears here. Example, *"If I mess up at work, I will be fired."* Or *"If I keep going out and drinking every night my wife will leave me."* Then below it list what action you could take to be better prepared.

Fear: _____

Action: _____

Fear: _____

Action: _____

Fear: _____

Action: _____

Fear: _____

Action: _____

Fear: _____

Action: _____

Feel free to do more☺!

In conclusion, courageous authenticity is always the best policy whether we are going through great or dismal times.

--

"We have to dare to be ourselves, however frightening or strange that self may prove to be." [1]

~ May Sarton

---

1   http://www.goodreads.com/quotes/tag/authenticity

Chapter 9

Finding Your Life Purpose

"Most of our faults are more pardonable than the means we use to conceal them."

~ François, Duc de La Rochefoucauld [1]

---

1   http://www.goodreadds.com/quotes/tag/authenticity

Finding Your Life Purpose

Courageous Authenticity Real Life Story: Reaching Out to Dad for Help

"A couple of years ago around the Christmas Holiday season, I was feeling extremely dissatisfied with my life and it culminated into a night of heavy drinking and drug abuse. By early morning, at about 7 o'clock, I ended up in a shady part of town looking to get more drugs. At this point I had a moment of clarity. I knew that the longer I prolonged this behaviour, the worse I would feel in the end. And judging by my immediate emotional state, it was going to be a nightmare, one which I was not sure I could handle.

Contrary to my usual plan of action, I decided that I must go to my father's house and come down. I proceeded to hail a cab and arrived at my destination shortly after. I paced around for a while in front of my father's building, trying to figure out what I would say to him.

I finally mustered up the courage to go upstairs and knock on the door. My stepmother opened the door and kindly invited me in, then went to the bedroom to tell my father I was there. My father awoke and came to talk to me, and I was totally up front with him and expected no sympathy. To my surprise, he praised me for coming over instead of continuing on my "trip".

We sat around and talked for a few hours and he told me that he was actually proud of me for being honest and seeking help when I most desperately needed it. The experience made our relationship stronger and showed me that I can finally, after all these years count on my father for support when I need it most."

~ Shervin F.

--

Life Purpose Overview

Now that your values are clearer we will complete another immensely powerful exercise that will create a powerful persona for yourself that transcends your ethnic background, age, sex, and profession. It will give you insight as to WHY you are on this earth and what your purpose is in life. This may seem grandiose or fanciful but it works and is one of the most powerful drivers to help you permanently live your life more fully and authentically.

A billboard I noticed on the highway sums it up very nicely:

"With clear purpose comes courage and direction."

The Life Purpose Statement (I will use LPS for short) will make every other difficult life question simpler, as well as help you to make choices that are much more aligned with your values and who you really are (developed in Chapter 6). It will help you to live courageously and authentically. Without knowing who you truly are or what your purpose is, HOW can you be authentic, let alone courageously so? In short, you can't.

Our life purpose is the thing we are meant to accomplish, the gift we are meant to bring.

I have found that on my life journey there have been many moments of confusion and angst around making critical life-changing decisions. Life is but a series of small and large decisions. A decision can be defined as action based on a choice. A decision cuts off all other options. Once I discovered and created my LPS, decisions definitely became much easier to make. This is why this exercise (which I explore with all my clients) is so important and meaningful.

--

Life Purpose = You Living To Your Maximum Potential

I have modified information from the book [1] I learned coaching through. The description summarizes the LPS exceptionally well.

"We say that people are born with a life purpose. Some people never look for their purpose, and so it remains unspoken their whole lives . But it is there. The life purpose is the reason we are on this planet. It is the thing we are meant to accomplish, the gift we are meant to bring. <u>Life purpose is NOT about a job or even an avocation.</u> It is the round-the-clock, 24 hour, every-day-of-your-life expression of who you are when you are reaching your full potential (what I call the Most Brilliant Self).

"When you are "on purpose" you are fulfilled. You are contributing and making a difference. When you are not on purpose, you feel discontented and unfulfilled. Even if you don't have an LPS, the life purpose is <u>still there</u>. Even if you can't articulate an LPS to your satisfaction, you still can tell the difference between when you are on purpose and when you are not on purpose. It is incredibly challenging for you to <u>NOT</u> act on this purpose. It feels terrible, dead and disconnected.

The LPS allows you to clarify your purpose in the world. Your LPS will be like a HUGE neon sign that will help you find your way out of the swamp when you are stuck. Because it is a personal statement for your own use, it can be as grand and sweeping or as transformational as you can handle. It is NOT open to the ridicule or judgment of others."

---

1   Whitworth, Kimsey-House (2), Sandahl, Co-Active Coaching: New Skills for Coaching People Toward Success in Work and Life, page 241

LPS Examples

The following are examples of Life Purpose Statements (LPS's), (notice the powerful visual and nature-related metaphors utilized):

"I am the lighthouse that guides people to their dreams."

"I am the dynamite that transforms people's lives."

"I am the rock in the shoe that causes people to remember they are alive."

"I am the alarm clock that awakens people to their magnificence."

This one is mine and it totally fits and motivates me two years later, even if it's a little long (ideal is less than fifteen words):

"I am the unstoppably fearless lion that demonstrates courage to dramatically wake people up to their Most Brilliant Selves."

Note that the LPS can and SHOULD be corny, grandiose, and flowery. All of that is okay. These are NOT for publication. **It is for you to fully feel the power of the life purpose in you**. Here I need to encourage you to challenge yourself to create a TRULY POWERFUL AND VIBRANT LPS! It is not something you will necessarily accomplish in this lifetime, but it should have tremendous, compelling power to motivate you to be in authentic and aligned action in your life and to stay purpose.

You can find inspiration anywhere to create your LPS; you can draw it, play music or write poetry, whatever works for you.

Live It: Your Courageously Authentic Life

Whatever inspiration you can find to help you articulate your LPS is good.

> **The Life Purpose Statement should be an anchor or lighthouse in a storm so you can access it when you are lost or off-course.**

Creating Your LPS

Here is how to create your LPS. I have made modifications to the exercise from the Co-Active Coaching book: [1]

1. I'll take you through four visualization exercises that generate impressions to allow you to gather insight about your life purpose.

2. You are to identify any and all common themes or patterns.

Examples: love, freedom, nature, passions, etc. Ask a close friend or partner to help you see the patterns. Once you have done the four visualizations, score each 1 to 10, 10/10 being perfect resonance and 1/10 meaning NO resonance. Resonance is when it strikes a chord for/in you and simply feels right. Reread the words to feel which ones connect deeply to you.

These words form the beginning of what is called an "impact statement". The initial impact statement is likely to be general: *"I want people to be happy."* or *"I want people to be in better relationships"* The problem with general impact statements like these is that they are too vague to motivate you to action. So you must go deeper as the LPS should be an anchor or lighthouse in a storm. You must be able to access and connect to it when you are lost or off-course in your life.

---

[1] Whitworth, Kimsey-House (2) Sandahl, Co-Active Coaching: New Skills for Coaching People Toward Success in Work and Life, pages 241-244

Ideally, it should describe the impact YOU WANT TO HAVE, such as having people embrace life, act authentically, see their true selves, find their personal power, discover their creativity, experience their magnificence, or return to aliveness.

3. Creating a metaphor that captures the life purpose. The format looks like this:

    "I am the_____(metaphor) so that people_____ (impact statement).

Live It! Activity #19: Create <u>Your</u> LPS [1] using the four visualization activities below.

--

Visualization 1: Imagine that you are in a large group of people milling about in front of a stage. Up on the stage is your Future Self (you in twenty years). Your Future Self begins to speak to this large group of people. Suddenly you become aware of a shift that has happened to you AND the entire audience. Your Future Self has in some way had a profound impact on you and on the rest of the people in the audience. You are all altered or changed in some fundamental way. Aware of this impact on yourself and the others, you leave the room altered for the rest of your life.

Questions:

What was the impact your Future Self had on you and the others?

How were you and the others transformed?

1   Whitworth, Kimsey-House (2), Sandahl, Co-Active Coaching: New Skills for Coaching People Towarad Success in Work and Llife, pages 243-244

Who was your Future Self BEING to have this impact?

Your notes: _____

_____

_____

_____

--

Visualization 2: Turn the clock back and look at a time in your life when you felt your full power – a time when your spine, arms, and fingertips were tingling with excitement – a time when you didn't care what anyone thought of you (you were 100% authentic and in flow) and you were absolutely alive!

Questions:

Where were you?

What were you doing?

Who was around you?

What was occurring in them at the time?

What was your impact on them?

Your notes: _____

_____

_____

--

<u>Visualization 3:</u> You have been given a HUGE billboard in your town/city. On this billboard you can write anything you want (a few words to be visible to drivers far away) and/or add pictures to impact the drivers (there will be thousands a day!). What would you write and what pictures and colours would you use?

Your notes: _____

_____

_____

_____

--

<u>Visualization 4:</u> You are getting into a rocket ship. The rocket ship takes off. You are on your way to an undeveloped planet in the universe. Let's call it Planet _____ (you're first name). It's a fine planet in every way, but it's uninhabited. You have the power to create this planet to be whatever you want it to be. When you land, what is it that <u>YOU ARE</u> going to make happen? What's the impact you want to have, that's going to form the planet the way you want it to be? The ship is landing on the planet. The door opens. You touch the planet and say, "It's going to be this way." What is "this way"?

Your notes: _____

_____

_____

Fantastic! Great work!

Now go over your notes above and determine what the main themes and ideas are that still deeply resonate and list them below.

_____

_____

_____

_____

To help you create your LPS, you definitely also want to consult your value statements in Chapter 6 for some inspiration.

"I am the _____ *(metaphor) so that people* _____ *(impact statement).*

Now think about the impact you want to have on the world. Is it more of a process (transformation, growth, authenticity)? Maybe an object (lighthouse, alarm clock)? An animal (lion, eagle, turtle)? Maybe it is a force of nature (wind, rain, sun, ocean, river, storm etc.).

Use evocative, juicy and transformative language that really connects to your core (Most Brilliant Self).

Give yourself some time to play with your LPS to fine tune it. Write it out and post it so you can see it.

Now that you have a powerful Life Purpose to guide you, saying YES and NO should come much more easily. Step fully into the greatest possible life you are here to lead.

--

"If you are always true, you do not need to remember anything you said or did in the past." [1]

---

1   http://quotesaboutbeingyourself.com/

Chapter 10

Authentic S.M.A.R.T Goal Setting

"How many cares one loses when one decides not to be something but to be someone." [1]

~ Gabrielle "Coco" Chanel

---

1   http://www.quotegarden.com/be-self.html

Authentic S.M.A.R.T Goal Setting

Courageous Authenticity Real Life Story: Just Fired? Take a Life-Clarifying Vacation!

"I had just been (shockingly and surprisingly) fired from a job I was very good at and enjoyed. I decided to take a one month life-changing vacation to Central America after losing my job, although it was difficult because of financial pressures (clock is ticking to find a new job, mortgage, pressure from parents/family, social pressure...).

I knew that the best thing for me was to clear my mind so I could start fresh and make the right decision (what do I want to do with the rest of my life?) and I can't even think right now!

When I sat in the interview for my dream job, the President asked me what I had done since I ended up finding my dream job. I answered that I took a one month vacation to find myself. He looked at me and realized I was the type of person that could handle whatever the job entailed. It came to me almost naturally, as if I had attracted it. I make more money now, am happier, work less and enjoy what I do. Had I not taken the time to clear my mind and reset, I don't know that this would have been possible." ~ Shawn C.

--

Goals That Feed And Motivate You

Now that you have discovered your values and your life purpose, it is time to begin learning to set powerful goals for yourself that are aligned with your greatest self. Setting goals aligned with your life purpose are the ONLY ones that will sustain you. Any goal contrary to your values or life purpose must be avoided. If it can't be avoided, limit it, because poor results will occur due to the scattered vibration and dissonance.

In my years as a coach I have realized that the two greatest challenges to goal setting are very surprising:

1. <u>Most people simply don't set goals.</u> It seems incredible, but most people don't have goals.

2. <u>Of the few that do set goals, their goals DON'T energize them.</u> Many people tell me they have goals. When I question and dig deeper, we both see clearly that their goals don't empower or energize them. Usually it is because the goal is too small or bereft of meaning. Think about it. If you set a goal of *"Making 10% more money next year,"* that goal has no juice! It has zero power or pizzazz.

If the goal becomes, *"Create a brand new internet distribution system that will save millions of lives!"* that has juiciness and heart. A goal needs to take your breath away; leave you a little dizzy by its image. Otherwise you won't stick with it. In my case, I love what I do, so work is pleasure for me as I choose what projects to get involved with. If they don't really jazz me, I say *"No thank you."*

Most people (including myself) hate traditional goal setting and dread the thought of creating lists of goals. Often, traditional goal setting feels like an exercise in frustration and drudgery. Someone has us list goals we want to achieve in _____ months/years and we are told to get excited about achieving them. No matter the intricacy of the goal attainment method or "system", if the goal is weak it will wither and we will fail.

> ## *Stop SHOULDING all over yourself!*

Well, it doesn't work as people usually pick goals that are too divorced from who they are and what they want. The list becomes an exercise in *"I should really want this, shouldn't I? Then why am I not excited about it?"* Now that you know your values and LPS you can more closely align your goals with what DEEPLY matters to you. That's exciting and the method we will use is exciting too. As I tell my clients often when they start with the "shoulds", *"Stop shoulding all over yourself!"* The following goal setting system is from CTI, Coaches Training Institute, where I apprenticed to be a coach. [1]

--

Motivation And Goal Achievement

I believe that most people aren't poor at achieving goals (through pure grunt work and pushing and grinding forward). In my experience people have:

a) <u>Poorly articulated goals:</u> Most people simply are weak at setting proper, well thought out, engaging and empowering goals.

b) <u>Impotent goals (weak or boring):</u> Not having big or juicy, *"Oh my God if I achieve this..."* giddiness. By goal I don't mean a daily activity like exercise, I mean a major life goal, something VERY BIG, something that will have a SUBSTANTIAL IMPACT in your life.

> ## *Who else will benefit when you achieve your goal?*

---

1   Coaches Training Institue (CTI) Co-Active Coaching Manual

Four Critical Goal-Setting Questions

Kehoe [1] mentions four questions to ask yourself when setting any goals. I feel the SMART technique we will use later captures all four:

1. <u>Why are you doing it?</u> Why this large goal? What is it about this goal that is important?

2. <u>Does it feel right?</u> Always trust your feelings. Find a goal that fits your subconscious. Ask yourself, *"Is this something I should be working on, and is it worthy?"* If it's good, the universe will send help.

3. <u>Is it a path with heart?</u> Making more money is NEVER a good goal. Find your passion! All multi-millionaires are extremely passionate about their craft! A major worthwhile life-changing goal can take years! For example when I coach, speak or write it feels so good, I prefer it to most of my other passions. When it feels that good it has heart.

4. <u>Who besides yourself will benefit once this goal is achieved?</u> Include as many people as you can think of, including your family or community. How can you include them? This will give you more inspiration and power to achieve. *"My success helps many people and my failure helps no one!"* My work impacts many people and that supports what I do as it helps others.

Most business texts discuss SMART goals but I feel (and CTI[2] as well) believe the last three letters (A, R and T) stand for different words.

---

1   Coaches Training (CTI) Co-ActiveCoaching Manual, Davies Black Publishing
2   Kehoe, John, "Mind Power for the 21st Century"Zoetic Books

Live It: Your Courageously Authentic Life

Powerful goals need to have five key components. These are the five letters in SMART. These stand for: **S**pecific, **M**easurable, **A**ccountable, **R**esonant and **T**hrilling.

Smart Goal Setting

<u>S</u>: <u>Specific</u>: Your goal has to be specific enough to motivate/challenge and jazz you up.

"I want to get fit" is vague and weak.

"I want to lose weight" is not much better.

"I want to lose 20 pounds by June, 1st" is better.

Best: turn it positive, *"I want to weigh 170 pounds or less by June 1st, so I can fit in my new 30 inch waist sexy pants."* That's great! Break the larger goal into smaller sub-steps.

--

<u>M</u>: <u>Measurable</u>: See above, to be measurable a date must be attached to a point (as discussed later) and ideally a numerical amount or percentage change.

--

<u>A</u>: <u>Accountable</u>: Someone needs to be your accountability partner. It could be a friend, spouse or a coach. A partner keeps you on task and accountable. This will reduce the odds that your STUMPS will sabotage you.

--

> *People who powerfully want a better life grow. They set unrealistic, big, hairy and audacious, resonant "<u>connected to their values</u>" goals with vision.*

<u>R:</u> <u>Resonant:</u> It needs to be connected <u>directly to your core (Most Brilliant) self</u> and your values (Chapter 6). Otherwise the STUMPS will ruin it quicker than you can say, *"Hey, what happened?!"*

Does this goal support your life purpose? Will it improve your life in many key areas you value? Look back to Chapter 6 to identify what values you honor in striving for and achieving this goal. Does it align with your LPS in Chapter 9? It should align with both.

People who want a demonstrably better life grow. They set unrealistic but big, hairy and audacious, resonant "<u>connected to their values</u>" goals with vision.

--

Your Subconscious Partner in Success

One of the greatest breakthroughs I experienced on my path to authenticity was this maxim from John Kehoe[1]:

"My Subconscious Mind is my Partner in Success!"

<u>It creates a critical concept (to manifest) in three ways:</u>

1. It confirms you have a "subconscious mind"!

2. A "partner" shares half the work with you, so you're not alone and can have some fun!

---

1 Kehoe, John, Mind Power for the 21st Century, Zoetic Books

3. It assumes you will be successful!

Repeat it to yourself multiple times a day until you know it at a cellular level! To help you, post it on your Vision Board!

--

T: Thrilling: The goal needs to literally scare you. Like, *"I had no idea I could do this! Wow! Wow!"* As a coach, I know where my clients' limits are and ask them to stretch so they grow and access all of themselves to get to the goal. You should set a goal that is too great to simply ignore, a game-changing, life-affirming goal that takes your breath away.

"Set goals not for the accomplishment of the objectives, but for who you will become in accomplishing them." ~ Jim Rhone

Striving and attaining goals builds our life container allowing us to tackle bigger and bigger and better goals. Goals that are connected to our essential selves (Most Brilliant Selves) are best.

California Dreaming

If I just look at the original goal I had set for myself: *"Live in L.A forever"*, I failed miserably since I lasted nine months (STUMPS perspective). However, I grew so much! If I reframe it to, *"I followed my dream and gave it my all and learned all the lessons I needed to!"*, then I succeeded. People who achieve greatness are great re-framers, changing meanings to positively support themselves and push themselves (and their lives) forward.

Powerful goals should be able to inspire you through the disappointing, difficult and scary times and let you stay the course no matter what. Even if you don't know the HOW or WHEN, that's ok. Now that you know the WHAT and the WHY , your Universal Manager can do the heavy lifting and orchestrate events in a way that over-achieves all of your goals easily and creatively.

--

Pick A Juicy Goal

You need a goal that you can get passionate, jazzed and (nervously) excited about. If it doesn't get you really thrilled (like a roller coaster) then keep tweaking it until it does.

Paradoxically and critically, <u>NOT putting a timeline on your major goal is much better</u> as it allows your Universal Manager to find better ways to achieve the goal than you could!

I found out the hard way that putting strict, short timelines on goals initially motivated me. However, as time advanced and progress wasn't very visible, I found myself giving up and losing motivation.

<u>I learned that: HOW and WHEN</u> IS NOT MY (or YOUR) RESPONSIBILITY!

Focus on WHAT you want and the powerful WHY you want it. A step further: SEE and FEEL great about it as if it happened already.

--

Live It: Your Courageously Authentic Life

<u>Three Ways To Attract (Manifest)</u>

There are three ways to activate the Law of Attraction [1]

1. <u>Visualize and FEEL something general:</u> *"I want a grey, late model, large luxury sedan."* Or *"I want a partner that shares my path of growth."*

2. <u>Visualize and FEEL Something Specific:</u> *"I want a white 2011 BMW 735i"* or *"I want to meet someone who is a teacher of life skills and an athlete."*

3. <u>Simply Feel Good!:</u> Just being in the higher vibrations (#1, Joy, Appreciation, Freedom, Love and Empowerment, #2, Passion, #3 Enthusiasm, Eagerness, Happiness) attracts great people, events and circumstances.

We often go upstream [2] when we perceive that our "stuff" is NOT COMING. Once we begin focusing on that ("Where is it? Why isn't it coming?"), we won't get it! Why? Because we are in Frustration/Irritation and Impatience, #10 on the ES. Meaning that we are out of the vortex.

For me, it's to have my kid's superhero dog story become a game-changing book series, movie and cartoon series by mid 2013! It's to have this book sell over 10,000 copies. It's to have 100 men's circles. Wow, those feel good!

--

---

1   Hicks, Abraham, "The Vortex"

2   Abraham Hicks term, meaning resisting the well-being current of your life. If the river of well being is lowing why would you want to go against the current by turning your boat upstream. All emotions below #8 are upstream as they don't feel good.

Big (Hard) VS. Small (Easy) Goals

Go BIG; go hard in terms of goals! As a matter of fact, bigger goals are easier as they have vision and people can get behind them at a grassroots level. A story to support this is from John Kehoe [1]: There was a man in a small town in Australia trying to raise $5,000 to renovate a kitchen in the village church basement. As hard as he tried he couldn't get people interested. Why not? Because it had limited vision, excitement and the townspeople couldn't clearly see their life changing for the better because of it.

The same man was in charge of raising $5,000,000 for a new library at the town college. People could see what a huge impact this would have on themselves and their community. The project was huge, had vision and mobilized everyone! The money was raised easily and quickly. So think of a huge goal with vision. Then people can help you and it will snowball.

--

My Greatest S.M.A.R.T. Goal Acheivement

I can't tell you how successful you will be implementing SMART goals, but I can give you my personal example. What follows is an example of my greatest success using SMART goal setting. When I decided on January 2, 2009 that we (Aida, her 2 kids & I) were moving to California, I had no job there and no papers. I did have an idea for a company, a potential E-2 visa, and an immigration lawyer. I was going to be there in six months!!! Insanity! Most around me, including most of my family, said it wouldn't happen because it was so crazy and unrealistic. Who supported me? My coach did. He and I determined that the worst case scenario was: *"I move down there, fail miserably learn a lot and came back to my teaching position, no harm or foul."*

---

1   Kehoe, John, Mind Power for the 21st Century

> *Once you have completed a ridiculous and impossible (to others maybe) stretch goal, you have grown and can tackle bigger and bigger ones.*

The plan was to take a sabbatical year off from teaching, allowing me to venture out on the tether but know I had a safety net if things didn't turn out. This way, it was a win-win situation. It was a SMART goal and we did everything required to get there.

We visited L.A., I put my condo up for sale and sold it. It was such a strong goal for my core values and additionally (critically) it had courage, vision and left me breathless (this is key, it must deeply capture your imagination)! It was a huge endeavor and project. We hit the June 30th milestone and it was one of my life's defining moments in terms of what is possible for me.

Once you have completed a ridiculous, impossible (to others maybe) stretch goal, you have grown and can tackle bigger and bigger ones (remember our life container - ship?).

Another critical piece is 100% authenticity. When I turned to Alana and told her we would be moving to California she began to weep. I asked her why and she said, *"I know when you say something it always happens!"* She was right. I rarely knowingly lie or exaggerate. I am a very good manifester and when focused, I can attract most things and experiences I set my intention on. Especially when they align with my Most Brilliant Self!

Integrity of your word is absolutely required. Otherwise, your subconscious mind will not believe you and not bring what you want to proper fruition. It does the heavy lifting, always finding a way to get to your goal. There is an almost unstoppable power and success vibration built into a specific, measurable, accountable, resonant and thrilling goal (SMART).

Live It! Activity #20: Look at your whole life. Develop SMART goals for each of your critical life areas on the Wheel of Life in Appendix 1 (Romance, Health, Money, Career, Fun, Family and Friends, Physical Environment and Personal Growth). Then watch your life hit the fast lane! Post these where you can see them (vision board)! Good luck!

Life Area   S.M.A.R.T GOAL

Family and Friends: _____

_____

Romance: _____

_____

Money: _____

_____

Career: _____

_____

Health: _____

_____

Fun & Recreation: _____

_____

Physical Environment: _____

_____

Personal Growth: _____

_____

S.M.A.R.T goals will accelerate your ability to live your ultimate life, a life with deep vibrancy, connection and authenticity.

"We are so accustomed to disguise ourselves to others that in the end we become disguised to ourselves." [1]

~ François Duc de La Rochefoucauld

---

1 http://www.quotegarden.com/be-self.html

Chapter 11

Media Inauthenticity: Powerful Limiting Beliefs

"Any life, no matter how long and complex it may be, is made up of a single moment--the moment in which a man finds out, once and for all, who he is." [1]

~Jorge Luis Borges

---

1   http://www.quotelady.com/subjects/being.html

Live It: Your Courageously Authentic Life

Media Inauthenticity: Powerful Limiting Beliefs

"Be your authentic self. Your authentic self is who you are when you have no fear of judgment, or before the world starts pushing you around and telling you who you're supposed to be. Your fictional self is who you are when you have a social mask on to please everyone else. Give yourself permission to be your authentic self." [1]

~ Dr. Phil

--

Courageous Authenticity Real Life Story: A Lot Less Weight = A Lot More Life

"A time in my life when I was courageously authentic was the moment I once and for all decided to lose weight. I was tipping the scales at 300 pounds, had no girlfriend, no sex life, low self esteem, and worst of all, terrible health. My entire family was overweight and seemed to be doing nothing about it.

I decided to take charge of my own life and do something about it. You have to open doors for yourself because they aren't always going to be opened for you. I got off the couch and into the gym. When my family would be eating greasy French fries and fish sticks for dinner, I would opt for a salad. When my family would be watching TV all night, I would be out jogging. I made it my own goal to get where I wanted to be and to have the body that I always only dreamt of.

With hard work, this dream became reality and after a year, I had dropped 100 pounds! Six years later, I currently still weigh in at a comfortable, muscular 220 pounds (I am 6 foot 4 inches tall!) and lead a continued lifestyle of healthy eating and exercise. I am

1 http://www.quotegarden.com/be-self.html

184

never going back to the person that I was. The positive physical and mental transformation of my life has helped put me on track to being the best person I can be, and it feels AWESOME."

~ Robert L.

--

Focused Powerful Beam Of Negativity

For every positive moment or inspirational story we see on talk shows, unfortunately there are dozens (hundreds or thousands?) of negative messages coming from the mass media. This chapter is centered around how the media is a generally very inauthentic, negative and yet disproportionately powerful force in our modern western culture. I won't even begin to worry about a conspiracy theory or if this is being created by some illuminati or hidden "Big Brother". It doesn't matter; it's negative and I don't need to constantly ingest it.

> ***What we focus on grows, what we resist persists and what we ignore haunts us no more.***

As a Law of Attraction practitioner and speaker I realize that: *"Anything we focus on grows, what we resist persists and what we ignore haunts us no more."* [1] As such, I want to say my piece in this section with the objective of allowing you to make your own decision on the place, type and impact you want media to have in your life.

Remember, your mind seeds [2] itself from your environment IF you don't actively feed it with positive and empowering

1   Maloney, Frank C., Cobra in the Closet, IUniverse

2   "Seeding your mind" is a Kehoe term signifying where we obtain our information.data that create our thoughts.

Live It: Your Courageously Authentic Life

(Empowerment, #1 on the ES) messages. There are many positives to media and I will also touch on those in an attempt to present both sides. Let's get the bad news over with first. TV is addictive and passive with others living their lives fictitiously as you stagnate passively. This quote sums it up nicely:

"Excess consumption of mass media can drain your positive energy and replace it with feelings of fear, hopelessness, dissatisfaction and inadequacy. These negative emotions suppress your vibrational levels by creating mental agitation, which leads to stress, which eventually leads to disease." [1]

Fear and Hopelessness are both at #22 on the ES, the lowest on the scale. Dissatisfaction and inadequacy are forms of Insecurity/Unworthiness, #21 on the ES; nasty and destructive indeed.

Nixing The News

I realized about six years ago how sensitive I was to media messages after I went through a tremendously difficult period in my life. While I was struggling, I found that watching the news at 6PM and again at 11PM was a substantial negative energy beam in my life. Once I realized I was in a position to make a choice, I made it. Then I stuck to it, and still do.

> *My results from cutting news out of my life were nothing short of miraculous*

I chose to severely limit all forms of news in my life for a period of one year to see the impact on my outlook and life.

Here's what I did: I got satellite radio for my car with no ads and great music. I listened to satellite radio at home and I stopped

---

1 "Raise Your Vibration, Transform YourLife!", page 70, James, Dawn, Lotus Press

watching all newscasts, including the community channel (the one that gives the weather, traffic and local news). I also stopped reading the newspaper. I did continue watching business-related news as I was (not anymore thank goodness!) also trading stocks (very unsuccessfully if truth be told!). I also, concurrently began listening to inspirational and motivational messages to feed/seed positive ideas into my thoughts.

Let's just say my results of nixing the news were nothing short of miraculous! I found an EXTRA ninety minutes a day to focus on what I wanted to do. My general mood also improved dramatically and any ultra-important/urgent news was relayed to me via other people anyway. To this day I have never returned to watching the news and don't plan on it.

Although my solution may seem radical to those who currently ingest (like a poison) a large quantity of news, it is an experiment WELL WORTH ATTEMPTING. I feel much of the success I have enjoyed is based on the fact that I control what I take (seed) into my mind as daily messages. It is as if I have created a moat around my mind that does not purposefully expose me to negative thoughts, ideas and vibrations. Being a very powerful empath, I need and thrive in environments with good thoughts, emotions and energy.

--

Things To Do With 90 Minutes A Day!

So, you want to take my "NO news" challenge? Good! I thought I would share what I did with that extra time to hopefully inspire you to find and benefit from the extra 90 minutes a day:

1. I began writing books because I felt I had something to say to

the world. I strongly felt I could make a deep positive impact on those I touched.

2. I began creating new projects that challenge me at the deepest levels I can handle and that often push me beyond my comfort zone. This is how I grew; I did things that seemed too big and difficult.

3. I began taking more chances and enjoying life more as I didn't fear the future anymore.

4. I began listening to a lot more motivational, Mind Power [1] and Law of Attraction philosophies as these new ways of thinking fit and mould my current world view almost perfectly.

5. I started reading books from great thinkers, philosophers and artists and also began meeting similar people via being open and abundant.

6. I regularly ran in the park, hit the gym more and became more present.

7. I rode on my motorcycle as often as I could to be in the best mind space I have been able to consistently achieve.

--

Some Suggestions For You

1. Watch nature shows on TV, preferably animals. Animals (and children) feel the emotion of fear but only based on ACTUAL real, threatening situations (a natural protective response to danger). Animals are NOT scarcity or fear-oriented as a default state. Many humans are. Once you live in fear (#22 on

---

1 John Kehoe term

the ES), you lose all creativity.

2. Connect deeply and playfully with children. They are also quite free of fear and rules. They feel, say and do what they want until their fear-based environment starts getting to them and they become as neurotic and worried as adults.

3. Connect deeply, curiously and reverently with golden agers. Many of them live very authentically and it is inspiring.

4. Get creative: paint, draw, write, journal, anything that allows you to process and interpret your human experience and life journey.

How can we be courageously authentic in our lives if we are always in fear and scarcity?: The answer: we can't.

Join one of my international videoconference men's or blended (men and women's) circles. We're there to support, grow and push each other.

--

Nasty News Messages

I began thinking about most of the news coverage that we ingest, like a toxin that numbs the taker into mild sedation in their lives. Let's look at a typical newscast in any major urban market. Then I will look at the topic and its resultant level on the Emotional Scale (Appendix 2).

Live It: Your Courageously Authentic Life

Read the following words aloud slowly and focus to see how they FEEL in your body and what emotions or visual scenarios come up.

War	Insurrection	Coup
Killing	Rape	Gang
Vandalism	Suicide	Theft
Volcano	Tornado	Hurricane
Landslide	Extreme heat alert	Global Warming
Arson	Crime	Devastation
Murder	Beating	Extreme Cold Alert
Earthquake	Destruction	Bankruptcy
Death	Violence	Tsunami
Fire	Fraud	

If you are like me, those words make you physically ill, and they SHOULD as they convey messages that are laced with fear, powerlessness, insecurity, guilt, rage and so many other low, "disconnected from source energy" [1] horrible-feeling human emotions.

How can we be courageously authentic in our lives if we are always in fear and scarcity? The answer: we can't.

Typical Newscast Emotions

Topics Covered in Newscasts:

Death

Death by suicide, murders, shooting, motor accident,

---

[1] Abraham Hicks term meaning completely diconnected from the abundant vortex (vibrational escrow) of the Universe.

aviation tragedy, gang and/or drug related, war, (and any other deaths I have neglected).

Death when seen by a normal adult would definitely create the emotions at the bottom of the scale:

#22 on the ES

Fear: Massive quantities of deaths would make a person fearful and rightfully so.

Grief: Seeing or hearing about people dying causes grief.

Depression: Death can make us depressed (an extreme form of learned powerlessness), as the accumulation of bad news creates a fear of the world and worry about what might happen next. That's not a good feeling!

Despair: Massive scarcity (death is the ultimate scarcity, a scarcity of life) will lead to despair. I believe that NOT realizing that the news is a false depiction of life is the biggest challenge for the masses. They seed their minds from a very negative and scarce environment. For every death by gangs there are thousands (millions?) of daily acts of kindness never celebrated or seen by many, although they do exist, I know I see them and do them. However, they do not exist in mass media's collective consciousness yet, and may never.

To be fair, the media's role is not to educate us and be our new value system.

Powerlessness: Constantly worrying about the grim reaper will give one a feeling of powerlessness.

Live It: Your Courageously Authentic Life

#21 ON THE ES

Insecurity: Death makes us feel vulnerable.

Guilt: Death creates guilt if a person wants to feel responsible. Some people are compulsive in wanting to be responsible for everything. By feeling responsible for media events people are not taking care of their issues and being present in their lives.

All the other emotions apply to death: Jealousy (#20), Hatred/Rage (#19), Revenge (#18), Anger (#17), Discouragement (#16), Blame (#15), Worry (#14), Doubt (#13), Disappointment (#12), Overwhelment (#11), Frustration/Irritation/Impatience (#10) and pessimism (#9) all apply.

As for emotions #8 to #1? Only the most psychopathic individuals would feel: Joy, Appreciation, Love, Empowerment and Freedom from constantly seeing or hearing about death.

Car Crashes

Some car crashes involve death and some involve "only" injuries. This topic would definitely cause fear, worry, doubt, and pessimism. When you watch the news and then get into your car, you are worried about people hitting you. When you are worried, you attract worry-worthy experiences like crashing into another car, etc. So we can agree that car crashes show us a world of death, destruction and dismemberment.

Fire

Fire also results in death, as well as family tragedies, which increase fear and worry. Some positive heroic stories are mixed in once in a while so as not to fully revolt the audience. Fire is a normal fear to have, IF AND ONLY IF it's actually happening right in front of you. It is not normal however to constantly worry about fire when it's not threatening.

Rape

Rape makes people fearful and insecure about the world they live in. Rape is a crime of powerlessness (#22) and rage or revenge (#19/#18). Someone feels they have been wronged or are frustrated with their apparent lack of control in their life. They act out and take control by removing someone else's freedom of choice via sexual assault.

Thefts/Vandalism

Thefts and vandalism represent a fear of loss of financial security and of freedom and loss of safety, which is definitely a scarcity-based perspective.

Plant Closures/Downsizings

Plant closures or downsizings depict the corporate version of kill or be killed. Watching the news and seeing all the companies that are closing stores or plants leads us to (falsely)believe that the world is falling apart. Worse, it feeds us a lie that tomorrow will be worse than today, which again, is a strong scarcity perspective and the definition of depression (#22 on the ES).

I won't continue going down the line as by this point it seems clear that the media has a very negative bias.

--

Future Present

I have heard and believe that depression is anger turned towards ourselves. Most people who get depressed (remember: labels are for jars, not people) have high standards and are very sensitive. The main thing I know is that when I feel depressed (upstream and disconnected from source energy), I feel and think thoughts that represents my tomorrow (future) as being worse than my today (present). This causes a feeling of powerlessness and despair (#22 on the ES).

The fact is all our power resides in the present moment.

The past is over and is only a reconstruction based on our individual psychological filters; it is not a fixed "reality". As such, I try as often as I can to reframe painful life experiences as powerful lessons and the path I had to take to be where I needed to go and feel what I needed to feel on my unique life path. The past is always open for more empowering (Empowerment is #1 on the ES) interpretations. Doing this is also a positively challenging thought exercise to keep your mind sharp.

We are always in control of our lives, our decisions, our actions and our persistence.

The future is but a dream, and without action, dreams become fantasies. The future is very appealing to us as it offers tantalizing limitless possibilities but it can lull us to sleep if we don't take action in the PRESENT to get to it. Therefore, the future is very powerful as our minds do need some great, fun, empowering things to inspire and motivate us to continue to do our best. If you want to remove a person's drive or mojo, keep convincing them the future is bleak and it is out of their control.

194

--

We Are In Control

The truth is much simpler. We are always in control of our lives, our decisions, our actions and our persistence. If we blame (#15 on the ES) someone else we are giving away our power and acting like a victim. Acting like a victim allows us to not be adult and mature, and it also stops us from feeling like we are in charge of our "ship" of life. Giving away decision power by blaming everything else than ourselves absolves us of responsibility.

The truth is that the media doesn't tell us about all the new jobs in technology, alternative and traditional energy and medicine, the financial markets, etc. If you feel like seeing abundance, look at a skyscraper! It took millions of dollars to create, it is semi-permanent, has thousands of offices and people working there. All the people who created it were abundant, the companies leasing it are abundant as are the people who work there, clean it, and supply all the office furniture.

Hollywood movies also present a dreamlike world where anything and everything is possible. A movie can't represent what hard work is and persistence like. Most movie scripts are understandable by an eight year old. This constitutes a dumbing down of society.

In an abundant universe, you shouldn't see others as competitors or enemies; see everyone as a possible collaborator in what you desire to create.

--

Media That Supports Or Promotes Authenticity

Now that I've completely lambasted the popular mass media, I want to complete the circle by appreciating (Appreciation is #1 on the ES) some media, as not all media is inauthentic.

Music

Of all media, I find music to be the most positive and authentic. I believe the powerful vibrations of music naturally raise our own personal vibration. If you are like me, depending on where you are on the vibrational scale, music meets you there and tends to amplify your emotion.

When you are in the upper emotions (#7 to #1), music sounds absolutely other-worldly and you may experience shivers and goose bumps. When you are low (#'s15- to #22), the opposite happens, and the music seems to attack you and bring you lower. I find song lyrics to be very spiritual and transformative. A quality songwriter's ability to take a life snapshot and put it to rhythm is unbelievable to me as I don't have that ability. This is Appreciation, #1 on the ES and it feels really good!

--

Live It! Activity #21: I challenge you to listen to lyrics and recognize and hear the brilliance I speak of.

--

Plays/Ballet

Very interesting and subtle messages are typically woven into plays and ballet, which offer life lessons and alternate perspectives

196

that are always good. Plays and ballets force us to think as they use and require plot development because they don't have the benefit (crutch) of post-production editing and high-tech computer graphics. The purity of the art form remains more present and powerful as the writing and characters carry the story.

--

Paintings

Paintings can also inspire a person to experience the full gamut of human emotions and show an artist's authenticity in sharing themselves and their perspectives on the canvas. Paintings are visual and create a magical window into another person's view of the world.

--

In summary, the media is a very powerful force and should be managed as any powerful force should be. Diligent care in limiting negative vibrations is critical to inform you in a balanced way. A powerful force needs to be respected and harnessed. Information from the media should never be taken at face value without examining assumptions, agendas and whether the framework is one of scarcity or abundance. Being aware of the difference between scarcity and abundance as well as the emotional scale will allow you to find the authenticity in media for yourself.

--

"Your time is limited, so don't waste it living someone else's life." [1]

~Steve Jobs

---

1 http://www.quotegarden.com/be-self.html

Chapter 12

Creating Powerful Thought Patterns

"The privilege of a lifetime is to become who you truly are." [1]

~ C.G. Jung

---

1 http://www.goodreads.com/quotes/tag/authenticity

Creating Powerful Thought Patterns

Courageous Authenticity Story: Creating Space in a Toxic Relationship

"My mother and I have always had a strained relationship. When I moved away to the big city, she stayed in our village. Over the years it became abundantly clear when I visited than I could never return to the limited opportunities and mentality of that place.

My mom and I had grown so different in key ways. Her ways of seeing the world and mine just didn't connect often anymore.

Our phone conversations were tense and aggressive. After years of trying to be a "good daughter" (trying to mend fences constantly) one night after I hung up it dawned on me. I was getting much more aggravation from our conversations than pleasure and realized that the relationship was now toxic.

I didn't do anything drastic, but my courageous authenticity allowed me to decrease the frequency of my interactions with the woman I loved dearly but simply didn't get along with. The quality of my life improved as I spent less time being angry and frustrated."

~ Jessica C.

--

Mind Power Material

Taking all that life has to offer DOES require considerable work on our parts. Training our minds to reduce/ignore thinking negative thought processes in favour of positive thought processes is essential to a great life. John Kehoe's materials in *"Mind Power for the 21st Century"* had a huge impact on my becoming courageously authentic. I strongly recommend acquiring this life and mind-transforming technology. His material is not motivational in the traditional sense. It allows you to train your mind to that of a modern day Jedi [1] (minus the levitation though, maybe I just haven't gotten there yet!). His material allowed me to fully embrace my very quirky AND infinitely talented self. Here, if your STUMPS got triggered it is because Passion, #2 on the ES can seem like cockiness to the uninitiated to the Emotional Scale (See Appendix 2). Kehoe has created six incredible laws that shed momentous insight into our truly limitless minds.

--

John Kehoe's Six Laws (With My Additions)

Law #1: "Thoughts are Real Forces!" A thought is a force and also an energy: it can be weak and scattered or focused and a powerful force. Since thoughts ARE REAL forces, we MUST, as often as possible, choose good thoughts!

Imagine if someone paid you $1 for each positive thought! You would have thousands of dollars a day (if you were positive) and then you would focus on positive thoughts! The truth is much greater than $1 a thought if you practice! If thoughts are REAL forces they can move things, people, ideas, and the world.

Do you see the limitless nature of this? Real forces aimed at ourselves (Depression, self-blame are STUMPS-created conditions) destroy our self-esteem, soul and our mind. Therefore, negative thoughts (which are real forces) must be identified and consistently dealt with. Kehoe describes <u>weeding</u> out negative thoughts <u>daily</u> as we would weed a garden. Otherwise they take over and you live a smaller than destined for life. We suffer when our STUMPS hijack and ruin our lives.

---

1 A Jedi is a mind master in the Star Wars (George Lucas)series, they can do magical things just with their minds.

Thoughts can be thought of as psychic knives. Would you aim a knife at yourself while dancing? No? Then don't do it with your thoughts! Thoughts are psychic knives that can injure or kill us and others. Respect your thoughts and treat them as the most important superpower you have, because they are. Psychic knives can build you a fortress, fortune or shelter, or mercilessly torture and kill you. These knives need serious training. John Kehoe provides this serious training.

--

Live It! Activity #22: What negative thoughts (psychic knives) do you habitually allow/encourage to fly around randomly in your mind?

_____

_____

Law #2: "The mind is a sending and receiving station of thought." The thoughts of others impact us, including anyone we are in contact with or live with, and what we listen to or watch on television. You can send out thoughts into the universe from this sending station. Like infrared or ultraviolet lights, science has simply not (yet) developed a way to measure the human mind's limitless power!

Science has however proven that negative thoughts can change the molecular makeup of gold and all other materials. A glass of water that has been impacted by negative thoughts has a jagged and disorganized molecular pattern. A glass of water impacted with positive, loving thoughts creates perfect crystalline structures. This is why Reiki healing can be performed from a distance. Thoughts and emotions are like light waves and travel at instant speed, I don't know how, but it works.

Law #3: "The Law of Attraction: thoughts that are emotionalized become magnetized." Thoughts that are positively or negatively emotionalized attract similar and like thoughts. Good thoughts attract other good ones, bad ones attract worse ones. But why stop at good? If we only have fourteen hours a day less all the hours we need to be focused on doing something like work, etc., that may only leave a few hours a day to really focus on what we want in our life. The most powerful emotions are #1 Joy, Freedom, Empowerment, Love, Appreciation and #2 Passion. When you feel these emotions you feel great and also powerfully attract other great thoughts, people and experiences.

Think strong, powerful and focused huge thoughts. Bigger thoughts and goals don't cost more! Your mind is like a movie, it DOESN'T know the difference between reality, a thought you think, or a movie you are seeing. Choose a good movie, choose good thoughts, and keep thinking them more and more often. Our minds can conceive a brick or a castle. Both require the exact same effort.

Goals are extensions of your thoughts. On my vision wall I have a saying, *"Big Goals are Easier."* Great goals also allow you to tap into inspiration from your heart.

> *Successful people consistently insert powerful, healthy, free, joyful and abundant thoughts into their minds.*

Law#4: _"The Law of Control: We are forever experiencing thoughts, but we have the power and the ability to either entertain them or dismiss them."_ If we have negative thoughts it is because WE ARE ALLOWING/TOLERATING them! We all carry so many bad, negative and hurtful thoughts. How long will you carry them? Any persistent negative thoughts are there <u>because you allow them</u>.

Be as concerned and focused on your thoughts as you are about your family, freedom, money and your health. If you become more concerned with the <u>QUALITY of your thoughts</u> (Inner World) than your current life situation, you will soon see massive changes in your Outer World (see Law #6). Look for relief from whatever negative thoughts/emotions you experience. That may mean watching comedy, going for a workout, a walk in the park, etc.

--

Law #5: _"The Law of Insertion: We have the power to insert any thought of any type into our minds."_ It doesn't <u>even</u> have to be real.

We are unlimited in our thinking.

Really successful people insert powerful, healthy, free, joyful and abundant thoughts into their minds. Combine this with Law #1 and you can see the power of this! You can see yourself doing, being anything YOU want. Think really big and really good thoughts because **YOU** are in control.

<u>An analogy:</u> Assume I tell you, you have the choice to see two movies. The first one is horrible but easy to watch because you know the storyline; it never ends well but it's familiar! The second one is exciting, dynamic and makes your heart soar. You leave the theater on fire. I don't know about you but I will watch the second

movie. Insert the best thoughts, the ones that have you getting to do, be or have what you want and HOW you want it.

You're the director of the movie in your head, which will create the movie of your life.

Choose empowering and exciting new thoughts and watch other great ones arrive to join them. Soon it's a great thought party.

--

Moving Up The Emotional Scale For Relief

Let's do an example of moving up the emotional scale (to feel better) via inserting new thoughts. I find working with an actual example works best in demonstrating how I moved up in a real situation that I experienced. Refer to the Emotional Scale (ES) if you want, it is in Appendix 2.

A few months ago a business associate with whom I do speaking engagements (where I sell my books) sat down with me and gave me devastating news. He said he had read my latest book and didn't like the message and content, and that he wouldn't help me to promote it anymore. This news literally floored me. My STUMPS immediately went crazy and imagined worst case scenarios. I had worked almost night and day for roughly a year to create the book myself, and I considered it my baby. And here was someone I respected saying that my baby was nasty, dangerous, undesirable, and not allowed anywhere near the events I was to speak at.

So my initial emotions were at the complete bottom of the scale (my nausea confirmed this):

Emotional Scale Level: **#22 Despair, Depression, Grief, Powerlessness, Fear**

Thoughts: *"I'm ruined. All the book sales are gone forever!"* (Note: extreme wording = STUMPS). *"I just ordered 75 of these, how will I sell them?"* (#22 Fear), *"I'm a loser and can't write!"*(#21 Unworthiness/Insecurity), *"How will I continue, maybe I should give up?"* (#22, Despair and Powerlessness), *"My baby is dead, Oh My God!"* (#22, Grief). Some drama here.

As I drove home I immediately began consciously moving myself up the scale, seeking thoughts that felt better (relief). With time and practice, this will become automatic for you too.

Emotional Scale Level: #19 Hatred/Rage and #18 Revenge

Thoughts: *"I hate that guy, what a jerk!"* (#19 Hatred/Rage) and *"I'll quit! That'll show him!"* (#18, Revenge)

A little later:

Emotional Scale Level: #15 Discouragement and #14 Blame

Thoughts: *"I have to start all over again. There's a year of my life gone."*(#15, Discouragement) *"Maybe if that woman hadn't called him to tell him what she really thought of the book, things would be different. Why can't people mind their own business?"*

I spent a couple of days at the Discouragement and Blame level. Then I had suffered enough.

Emotional Scale Level: #11 Overwhelment and #10 Frustration/ Irritation/Impatience

Thoughts: *"I've got two other books I'm working on. Which one should I focus on? I can't decide!"* (#11, Overwhelment) and *"How long will THAT take to write? I'll be 8-12 months without anything to sell at my speaking engagements! Why should I do them then?"* (Impatience/Frustration/Irritation)

A day or so in these emotions then:

Emotional Scale Level: #8 Boredom

Thoughts: *"I don't feel like doing anything, I'm bored."*

Emotional Scale: #6 Hopefulness

Thoughts: *"Maybe, I can sell my other books!"*

Emotional Scale: #4 Positive Expectation/Belief/Faith and #2 Passion

Thoughts: *"My next book will be amazing and I can write it in no time and can sell it by summer!"* That was the genesis of "Live-It!".

Emotional Scale: #1: Empowerment, Freedom, Appreciation, Joy and Love

Thoughts: *"This will make me an even better writer and my future success that much more meaningful and triumphant."*

> *You are not aware that your Inner World ceates your Outer World of circumstances.*

Live It: Your Courageously Authentic Life

It took me a few days but I managed to get myself up the scale working away on this book, making it happen. Be gentle with yourself at first, any jumps of over three levels are uncomfortable and don't usually work. Try it. You will know you went too high, too quickly, if it bounces you back down the scale. Of the top #1 emotions, I find Appreciation the easiest to access when I'm lower down the scale.

--

Live It! Activity #23: I challenge you to try moving up the scale yourself on a topic of your choice. From now on, ACTIVELY choose the best and most empowering thoughts. Here's a trick, if you wouldn't be motivated to see a movie based on these thoughts, reach for relief using the ES!

--

Law #6: "The Law of Connection" The Inner World (of thoughts in our mind) and Outer (circumstances and events) world are connected. You are already quite aware that what happens in the Outer World reflects and impacts your Inner World, depending on the meaning you give the event (Outer World) in your mind (Inner World). You will react based on that interpretation. That is why Zen masters and monks always preach inner calm; from calm emanates creativity and resourcefulness.

> **_Life isn't what happens to you, but the story you make up about what happened to you._**

Emotional State Requirements

Your emotional state at any time is based on three things:

1. **Your Physiology** - try being depressed standing, chest out, shoulders back and smiling, you can't!

2. **Your Language** - What you tell yourself, how you reframe events.

3. **Your Beliefs** - If you believe you can, you're right! If you believe you can't, you're also right!

You are probably <u>NOT</u> aware that Your Inner World creates your Outer World of circumstances.

That is the beauty of this law. You see events outside you as noise, but they don't get to you. You know in your Inside World what is important to focus on and you keep focused and move towards your dreams. You become like a dog on a bone, focused and determined AND having fun doing it. However, you are still flexible with your life (Outside World), and a new prioritizations occur leading to more alignment to your Most Brilliant Self.

Many people give all of their attention to the Outside World of events (their lives) and are emotionally tossed about like a cork on the ocean. They don't feel good. How can you feel good if your happiness is based on "random, outside of you not in your control", life events? As mentioned earlier, your thoughts are much more important than your circumstances.

I now give much less real thought about the Outside World except to live my inner world agenda which is always first. Once you become more adept at doing this, it is really quite miraculous. It is as if you are in control of your thoughts, your thoughts are not controlling you! Remember, **"Life isn't what happens to you, but the story you make up about what happened to you."**

Live It! Activity #24: Write these six laws in your own writing (to assimilate and believe) and post them as many places where you see them constantly (ideally, your vision board). You need to review and repeat these laws to yourself EVERY DAY for a minimum of 60 to 90 days. Don't let the STUMPS convince you otherwise. Part of mind training is following through and doing it despite the STUMPS' unlimited GREAT REASONS NOT TO DO THEM.

--

Your thoughts create your life.

Don't let intellectual understanding ever fool you, you will know when you actively choose every thought inside yourself. Since the inner and outer worlds are connected, by extension the world will vibrate with you at that high level. Then and only then will you truly have understood. You need to think this EVERY day as that's how it becomes a CELLULAR part of you. Similar to learning multiplication tables, repetition is key. You will know when you get it.

These six laws when applied in unison have a huge positive and empowering impact on your thoughts which impact your emotions. As we have covered, your thoughts create your life. Better thoughts will bring a better life, it's that simple. Train your mind to be better at thinking, imagining and visualizing. Your potential will be limitless and you will be able to live your most courageously authentic life.

--

"Like the sky opens after a rainy day we must open to ourselves... Learn to love yourself for who you are and open so the world can see you shine." [1]

~ **James Poland**

---

[1] http://www.quotegarden.com/be-self.html

Chapter 13

Challenges to Living-it!

"Be what you are. This is the first step toward becoming better than you are." [1]

~ Julius Charles Hare

---

1   http://www.quotegarden.com/be-self.html

Challenges to Living It!

As is the case with all worthwhile journeys and endeavours, there are challenges to living a courageously authentic life. I discussed at length in Chapter 3 how our STUMPS is the #1 deterrent to living authentically. Our (untrained and negative, media-seeded) own minds cause most of the impediments to a life of courageous authenticity. Correction, a part of our own minds, the same way our foot is NOT us, our STUMPS is not us, but it is a part of us. As I tell many of my circle members and coaching clients, "You need to start getting out of your own way." It is a difficult concept to really understand and accept at a deep level, but our minds are both our biggest saviors AND our enemies, sometimes at the same time!

Without the proper and consistent training provided by a mind power development program such as John Kehoe's *"Mind Power for the 21st Century"* [1], our minds are basically like small boats tossed asunder like a cork in a tumultuous ocean. I am not exaggerating. the average person's mind is akin to an unruly teenager's, who focuses on whatever is of its interest with no rhyme or reason other than whatever emotion is being triggered by the Outside World of events and circumstances (our environment). Most people have never been told or taught that unlike the weather, we can choose the thoughts we think and change our focus to improve their quality. That said, there can (and probably will) be significant and persistent external resistance to choosing to live your life with consistent authenticity. It requires diligence, persistence and courage.

Let's investigate the impediments to Living It!

---

1   Kehoe, John, Mind Power for the 21st Century, Zoetic

> *The people we spend most of our formative years with,*
> *our parents, definitely have the biggest impact on what*
> *we experience and what values we sepouse.*

External Impediments To Living It

Family

Family includes anyone we are in relationship with via blood lines and anyone connected to our blood lines by law. Additionally, anyone we emotionally value or consider family, even without blood line connection. These include your mother and father, siblings, aunts and uncles, grandparents and cousins as well as all manner of in-laws.

Parents

As the people we spend most of our formative years with, our parents definitely have the biggest impact on what we experience and what values we choose to honour. As such, they can be one of the biggest impediments (even as we become adults) to living as our fully authentic selves. Why? Our parents are human too with their own fears, dreams, emotions and negative personality traits (their STUMPS). They come from a generation that knew war and poverty, so many of them have a scarcity perspective of life (discussed in detail in Chapter 2). As such, often fear and worry permeate their life and world view. They have created their own masks and ways of being that are pleasing to others but divorced from their truth. Because of this, there is a lot of emotional charge to having their progeny **"actively pursuing"** their own truth. This is because they instinctively take responsibility and self-blame for how their kids behave or misbehave.

In my personal experience, many people misunderstand my

213

actions when I am authentic. They believe I am actively out to hurt them or am being rude or disrespectful. They also often think I am a rebel or shit disturber, which in all honesty I sometimes can be!

> **Remember, if we are empty, we have nothing to give others.**

Our parents are also often the last ones to see us as we are now, as opposed to how they remember us. They still see themselves changing *"little Johnny/Sally's"* diapers! They have not fully understood, let alone accepted, who we have become as adults.

In my case, I always strive to be clear in my intentions and explain why I am doing certain things to live my truth. I also try to be as respectful as possible in the way I act so that other people will at the very least have an opportunity to see I did not actively set out to hurt them.

It is also important to realize that when someone is hurt by something we do or say, it is always <u>THEIR</u> unresolved issues that are being triggered. For example, if someone tells me I am selfish, I now agree with them, and inform them that being selfish is the only way for me to take care of my needs. Once my needs are satisfied, I have exponential amounts of energy, passion and joy to give to help others. If we are empty we have nothing to give others.

Additionally, if I realize that I have done something that was out of line, I admit it and apologize for it, not only for the other party, but so that I will stop carrying the Guilt (#21 on the ES).

> **Your siblings also are probably not crazy about you ACTIVELY living your truth so clearly.**

I think that in the majority of cases, it is safe to say our parents want what is best for us. They truly want to save us time and suffering by informing us about all that could happen. They project their hopes, fears, dreams, worry and generally all of their own unresolved psychological issues on us. So if your parents had to work hard in commission sales or as entrepreneurs, they often want you to have a university degree (nothing wrong with those I have 2!) and/or a cushy, corporate job so you can have a better or easier life than they ever did. Their intentions are good but the reality is that only WE OURSELVES know what is best for us and we have to make our own choices, experiences and mistakes.

--

Siblings And Extended Family

Similar to parents, our siblings and extended family carry a lot of weight in terms of their influence on us. They are also probably not thrilled about you living your truth this clearly. It is very confronting and destabilizing to have a brother, sister or cousin, suddenly become free of the many (artificial and inauthentic) constraints that bind and saddle most people.

People may actually actively discourage you from living the path of authenticity. Remember, they have their own inauthenticities that they may or may not know exist. Their fears (#22 on the ES) and worries (#14) and doubts (#13) will definitely surface as they admonish you (openly or behind your back) for your behaviour BECAUSE THEY MAY be Jealous (#20 on the ES)! They may even go further and start ignoring you or not returning your emails or phone calls! This in itself is enough of a deterrent for most people to cave in and return to wearing their inauthentic masks even if they don't like to.

> *I strongly believe that those who are the most fulfilled in life are those who a) know what their needs are and b) are proficient at getting their own needs met.*

Family is a very unique group because unlike all the other people in our lives, they are of our blood. You can change friends, employers, neighbours, partners, etc., but family is permanent. This is why I believe some people eventually cut off ties with their families as they just can't deal with what they perceive to be a relationship that creates more harm and pain than it delivers in love, safety and connection. This may seem like an oversimplification of relationships but at its core I believe it is highly valid. Many more stay in toxic family relationships. A better solution is to be authentic and see what happens.

--

The Six Human Needs

When we look at our lives, our main focus (whether we know it or not) is to get our needs met. These needs are the Six Human Needs posited by Tony Robbins.

Six Human Needs:

1. Certainty

2. Variety/Uncertainty (the opposite of Certainty)

3. Significance

4. Connection (the opposite of Significance)

5. Growth

6. Contribution

Those who are the most fulfilled in life are those who a) know what their needs are, and b) are proficient and authentic (transparent) at getting their own needs met. Of course we should all meet our own needs WITHOUT impeding others from meeting theirs. In my previous example of someone cutting off their family they may perceive/feel (remember our perceptions are our realities) that a) they are certain their family hurts them, b) their family provides variety but perhaps it is negative, c) their family does not make them feel important or significant, d) they feel the connection to their family hurts them, e) they feel stifled by their family (can't grow) and f) they feel they can't or don't want to contribute.

--

Life Partners/Significant Others

A great relationship built on trust, honesty and open communication will absolutely thrive once both partners embrace and begin living authentically. The amount of freedom (#1 on the ES) that is in an authentic relationship is difficult to understand unless you have lived it. As I am also quite new on this authentic path, my current relationships are completely and utterly different (and infinitely better) than the ones I used to have.

> *Sexual intimacy is also drastically improved as both partners actually say what they want, like, or don't like.*

Ironically, those who have failed at love are much better at love than those who have succeeded. Another of life's strange paradoxes! Becoming authentic makes you deeper.

"You CAN'T love deeply until you are a deep person in the first place, and the torture of difficult love is the very ordeal that makes you capable of strong love. Your love for another, especially when it is difficult or impossible, works on you and prepares you for a different way of loving." [1]

Being able to be myself more consistently (ego always has a way of showing up!) has allowed many amazing and beautiful connections to blossom quickly, easily and solidly. It has also pushed quite a few people away (their closeness was obviously not based on anything solid and lasting). There is no such thing as a permanent relationship in my opinion. Relationships can be thought of as sharing a portion of our life's road with another person as long as both choose to.

Everything in your life is transformed with authenticity. Communication is clear, direct and meaningful. Conversational exploration is unlimited, bold and adventurous. You can share freely what is happening for you and what you are feeling. It short circuits much of the resentment and anger that builds when couples are inauthentic (often by not clearly communicating their feelings with each other). Arguments are shorter, cleaner and less dramatic, if they even occur.

Sexual intimacy is also significantly improved as both partners actually say what they want, like or don't like. Making love becomes an incredible experience filled with wonder and freedom of expression. It requires checking the ego at the door as many of the problems we experience in relationships stem from our egos being bruised or threatened (unresolved previous hurts). Whenever our egos are threatened it is a good idea to ask ourselves why we are threatened and share it with our partner, as this will help them to help and understand us. Being authentic always builds trust which

---

1   Moore, Thomas, Dark Nights of the Soul, page 138, Gotham Books.

is the powerful bond that keeps a couple together through thick and thin.

> *Being authentic guarantees you will have more powerful friendships based on the fact they really like you and not some embellished or photoshopped version of you!*

Authenticity Risk

There is one risk (totally worth taking by the way) in all of this and that is that you choose authenticity and your partner DOES NOT. If that happens, a few different scenarios will play out.

Scenario 1: Gradually your partner will begin to appreciate your authenticity and will gradually become more authentic themselves which will lead to the previous wonderful scenario of the "authentic couple in an authentic relationship" (scenario previously described).

I have no idea what the odds are of either of these two scenarios occurring.

Scenario 2: Your partner starts using your authenticity against you or resenting you. In that case, at some point it is best to exit the relationship as it is impossible to build a solid relationship when only one party is being open and real. Becoming authentic can be seen as a "fast forwarding" of the relationship for both good and bad.

An example of authenticity occurred a few months ago when a person I had been seeing for a few months (who is now my girlfriend) asked me directly, *"What is it we have?"* or *"What is this relationship?"* So she was being authentic in saying she was wondering (perhaps worried or curious) where we were in terms of our relationship.

In the past, my fear (#22 on the ES) of being alone (human need #4, Connection) would have persuaded me to lie about wanting a long term relationship and being serious in the hopes she would deem me a worthwhile relationship risk/investment. This time was different as I spoke my truth and said, *"I'm still not really sure what I want but I enjoy the time we are together and am open to seeing where it goes."* As I said those words a terrible fear struck me that she was about to reject me or get angry and storm out (our STUMPS can be quite the drama king/queen!). Amazingly, she looked puzzled for a moment and then said, *"You know what, I'm confused too and don't really know what I want."* This was a revelation for me as I realized the power of authenticity, honesty and speaking my truth. The relationship really strengthened after that as we both enjoyed what we had instead of wondering what it was, might or might not be.

I am still in this incredibly fun relationship and it is a very solid and connected relationship of equals. It is quite different from most of my past relationships which would be difficult mostly because of how rigid I was being.

--

Live It! Exercise #25: What important conversation do you NEED to courageously have in the most authentic way? If you can't then you must! Will you? What is the cost if you don't, to YOU? To HIM/HER? I challenge you to see the power of authentic honesty.

--

Friends

Friends, especially close ones, also have a powerful impact on how we act and what we do. Many of them (not all) will also resist authenticity, sometimes due to the same reasons our family does. Being authentic in who you are *guarantees you will have more powerful friendships* based on the fact they really like you and not some embellished or photoshopped version of you! These kind of friendships last as they are built on real affinities. Ironically, it becomes much easier to develop powerful friendships (and all relationships) when we are our true (Most Brilliant) selves.

Existing friendships may disintegrate when you embrace authenticity as they may have been based on you being and acting in nice but inauthentic ways. This is a price that MUST be paid to be true to yourself. I find it easier to believe the friendship wasn't real anyway as anything that is meant to be simply is and it's easy. Friendships you constantly have to "work" on are not the good types to have. They drain your energy. Great friendships happen naturally.

Neighbours

Neighbours can often become friends yet they have their own fears, hopes and dreams and jealousy can pervade these relationships too.

> *Remember, if someone gets triggered by you, it's their stuff (unresolved issues) that comes up.*

Coworkers

Coworkers are a particularly interesting challenge as they can run the gamut from mortal enemies to great friends.

Live It: Your Courageously Authentic Life

Unfortunately, the office/work environment is by nature a competitive and jealousy-inducing place (low vibration, at #20 on the ES). Once you start really becoming your authentic self, many will be threatened as they will feel exposed or small. Remember, everyone gets triggered by you, but it's their stuff, a.k.a. unresolved issues that come up. It's never about you! Once you understand that,

"It's none of your business what other people think", you are on the right path!

Authenticity will create changes in all of your relationships, beginning and ending with yourself. Stay the course and know that authenticity is the only way to really live fully!

--

"You must have control of the authorship of your own destiny. The pen that writes your life story must be held in your own hand." [1]

~ **Irene C. Kassorla**

---

1   http://www.quotegarden.com/be-self.html

Chapter 14

Best Practices to Grab MORE Life ALL THE TIME

"The most important kind of freedom is to be what you really are." [1]

~ Jim Morrison

---

1   http://www.quotegarden.com/be-self.html

Best Practices to Grab MORE Life ALL THE TIME

TOOLS TO ACHIEVE AUTHENTICITY

In this final section, I have sought to share some tools to allow you to become more courageously authentic. Remember, these are all tools that have worked for me, so go over them and use what you like. There is NO right or wrong way to become more courageously authentic, in my humble opinion. Any activity, technique or exercise that allows you to accept, like and then eventually love yourself more is a powerful one on your journey of courageous authenticity.

Self-Acknowledgements [1]

Self-acknowledgements are absolutely critical to begin the process of truly valuing yourself, raising your vibration level and giving your subconscious positive images of you to create when you sleep. John Kehoe advises creating fifteen to twenty things that make you feel good AND successful. They should be about WHO and WHAT you are NOW (not hope to be).

Nothing succeeds like success! Start vibrating success energy. [2]

What this activity does is CREATE a VIBRATION of Success (via self-love, self-appreciation, self-empowerment and self-respect). Appreciation, Love and Empowerment are all #1 on the ES at the top of the scale! This activity ensures you achieve and maintain a vibration of success. Think of this list once it is posted as positive advertising for yourself. This exercise is important because it counteracts one of the nasty ways in which our mind works.

---

1 Kehoe, John, Mind Power for the 21st Century, Zoetic

2 Kehoe, John, Mind Power for the 21st Century, Zoetic

Typically, whenever we achieve something, no matter how great, we forget about it and focus on the next thing we want to achieve. **"This "leaks" critical "success vibration"**, Kehoe says.

Look at them and read them for a few minutes every day. I started putting them on my vision wall and it works. Once I began they just flowed. The key is to pick something that is TRUE ALREADY, and NOT what you hope to be. Otherwise your sticky negative sidekick the STUMPS will question it. These are just for you, so be real and edgy. Use short sentences with powerful and emotionally evocative language for maximum impact when reading.

Here is my list to help get your juices flowing:

Frank's Self-Acknowledgements

1. I'm an attentive and loving dog owner!
2. I'm a fantastic lover!
3. I'm a motivator and leader of people!
4. I'm a powerful and exciting teacher!
5. I'm a world-class coach!
6. I am a prolific and great writer!
7. I have the creativity of an artist!
8. I'm exciting and passionate!
9. I touch people in caring ways!
10. I'm a great motorcycle rider both on and off road!
11. I'm an opportunistic experimenter!
12. I am very adaptable!
13. I love and am always trying new things!
14. I am fearless!

15. I'm a very smart (EQ) person!

16. I'm a (damn) sexy man!

17. I'm a man of great vision, integrity and soul!

18. I am a doer!

19. My word is my bond!

20. I have immediate access to my powerful intuition!

21. I have a HUGE range of feeling!

--

Live It! Activity #26: Your turn: I <u>challenge you to come up with YOUR 20 self-acknowledgements!</u> Go for it! Put them on your vision board (see Chapter 7: Vision/Dream Boards). You need to see them regularly. They stump the STUMPS!

<u>You Must Believe It Or Don't Write It. It Won't Work!</u> Sorry for the shouting! If you question one, change it so it feels true. You need to be sure it fits!

Your Self-Acknowledgements

1. _____

2. _____

3. _____

4. _____

5. _____

6. _____

7. _____

8. _____

9. _____

10. _____

11. _____

12. _____

13. _____

14. _____

15. _____

Spend five minutes a day feeling that you are successful now which will in turn attract more success (since similar vibrations attract each other powerfully).

As with all habits it will take a solid four weeks of doing something for it to become a habit.

2.   Visualizations

Positive visualization of the future is an incredibly powerful manifesting technique. As we have already discovered, our subconscious minds don't know whether a movie is being played on a movie screen or life happening or if a thought is being thought. So if we choose to play positive movies (visualize positive experiences and outcomes), the subconscious believes that is reality and will work triple time orchestrating events subconsciously that will lead to that life.

During the night as you sleep, your subconscious mind goes into processing mode to figure out what it will do to achieve the successful environment and people it experienced, saw and felt in the positive visualizations. At first it will be difficult but you must force yourself with the same diligence you would use to go to work out at the gym. As with all habits, it will take a solid four weeks of doing something for it to become a habit. Soon, you will constantly see very positive future scenarios in all areas of your life and expect them to happen, and soon they will happen for real.

Once that happens, (#4 Positive Expectation, Belief, Faith), you are seriously pulling in amazing people and experiences as you revel in this incredibly "best case scenario happening every day matrix-connected" world you live in and create. Once your visualizations (supercharged with vision boards of course!) start to come true, your confidence increases and you take more chances with being your true self. It is a positive self-reinforcing loop. Most people experience self-reinforcing loops of negative thoughts. That is what depression is, a negative loop of pessimistic thoughts that attract other pessimistic thoughts (Pessimism, #9 on the ES).

Visualizing sets a new program in your mind, and you must believe (and more importantly feel) that the visualizations **WILL** work for them to work. Better yet, **FEEL** as if they have already happened.

As Henry Ford said:

"If you think you can do a thing or think you can't do a thing, you're right."

--

3.   Vision Boards

Covered extensively in Chapter 7.

Many couples argue just to experience some emotional tension, no matter what it is.

---

4.   Managing (Minimizing) Negative People/Environments

We are who we associate with. Whoever we interact with either uplifts us or brings us down. Some give us energy some take it away. People with negative outlooks on life should be eliminated or at least reduced. You have to surround yourself with successful, excited and **"passionate about their lives"** people, otherwise they take your passion.

We all need to feed and be fed. Think of us as emotional/ spiritual vampires. We get our "juice" (energy/passion) from others and others get their juice from us. We create our own juice by thinking positive thoughts and being in (#1 and #2, Appreciation, Joy, Freedom, Love, Empowerment and Passion) great spirits. Some want our positive juice as they are depleted (negative thinking depletes you and your health). **Many couples argue just to experience some emotional tension, no matter what it is.**

Like attracts like and if you are with people who take from you, you will lose as they will drain you. Only if you begin associating with those at your level of vibration (or above) can you grow. Think about it. Who do you get better at playing tennis with, a beginner or an expert? Even if the expert destroys you, you play better because the game is at a higher level and you are learning from a master.

The number one predictor of future success for college graduates is who they associate with, NOT their grades, degrees or anything else...who they associate with. Pick your friends and associates with extreme care. Why? Your future life quality depends on it.

You can't Live It! if people around you don't have anything to support you (they are empty)!

> *All you are responsible for is the WHAT you WANT and WHY you want it. Your job is to allow.*

5.   Become Disturbed Enough To Make Change Mandatory.

Only, when you become really disturbed about a problem will you be motivated to act on it. So the trick is to increase your standards dramatically as you will get disturbed much sooner and be motivated much more. When you are very disturbed, it gives you the leverage to push yourself to change and improve.

Contrary to popular lore and belief, suffering is optional in this life.

If you suffer, you must take responsibility for suffering as a result of your own (predominantly) negative thoughts. Once you accept 100% responsibility for everything - I mean EVERYTHING in your life - then you are in control because everything depends on YOU. There are NO external forces or negative events. Of course, you ONLY focus on only what you can control. All you control is your thoughts and actions.

Law of Attraction-wise, all you are responsible for is the WHAT you WANT and WHY you want it, so make it awesome, juicy, fun and passionate. Your universal manager (mine is called Mike) will handle the HOW and the WHEN. So now you can stop worrying about them and really spend your time on **WHY you want WHAT you WANT** and watch it fly in so quickly that your head/life will spin. The Universe wants to send you what you desire but the order MUST be clear and consistent.

--

6.   Integrity Is Key

It will help immensely to get you disturbed if the people you associate with are on a similar path of self-improvement. So increasing your standards in the people you spend time with is key to sustainable success. People of a higher standard will improve you as you learn from them and are pushed to be better.

To enjoy maximum leverage when disturbed, you ABSOLUTELY NEED to have 100% integrity. That will ensure that when you tell yourself you will lose 30 pounds, your subconscious believes you, otherwise it won't work. Your STUMPS will say, *"Lose 30 pounds? How many times have you said that before and did NOTHING!"*

And he/she is right. If you lie, your subconscious doesn't believe you so ALL your conscious work will go to waste. Stop lying (all forms from exaggeration to little white lies to standard lies) today, and watch your life change. It will be utterly stunning to those uninitiated with the power of integrity.

--

7.   Minimize Negative Media Vibration

Covered extensively in Chapter 11.

> **Curiosity is the key to greatness and fulfillment. Once we realize we really know very little (at a cellular level, not just intellectually), that is when wisdom begins.**

8.   Develop "Crazy Grandpa" & "Kid" Courage

We all have that "crazy" uncle, aunt or grandparent that says exactly what they think. They embarrass other family members by their straightforward and brutal honesty and lack of apparent social couth. Why do they act this way? Kids are still connected to source energy and know what feels good and don't think about it.

As for older folks, perhaps because they have been through life and realize that they don't have much time left and they refuse to bow to convention. They simply don't care much about what others think or say. That's why they are a riot at family gatherings! You never know what they will say and it is so fun. Kids below the age of six are similar. They haven't been "brainwashed" yet by society's often ridiculous conventions of what is right or wrong and how to live. Children's curiosity is powerful and they follow it.

Curiosity is the key to greatness and fulfillment. Once we realize we really know very little (at a cellular level, not just intellectually), that is when wisdom begins. Because once you are fully open you realize the greatness and absolute limitlessness of our world. Then you are like a sponge and just bloom as a person as the wonder of this life begins to amaze and fully engage you. You spend your time in Appreciation, Love, Joy, Empowerment and Freedom (#1 on the ES). Life is in flow and utterly passionate (Passion: #2 on the ES).

> ***Begin by raising your standards of acceptable behaviours from others.***

---

9.   Begin Surrounding Yourself With Authentic People

Once you begin the journey/odyssey of authenticity, it can be a lonely road as your existing network and the media consistently shove inauthentic role models in your face (and worse, your mind). **Begin by raising your standards of acceptable behaviours from others.** When someone crosses that line, it is your authentic response that will set the tone. Without being aggressive, simply call out the behavior, its impact on you, and that it doesn't meet your standards. If the same person does it again, **your job is to love yourself enough to walk away and/or tell them why you are leaving.**

--

Hopefully these tips will be useful for you in living and embracing your most authentic life.

--

"Being authentic is the ability to be true to oneself. Living an authentic life requires the ability to be true to our own wants, needs and desires and not live our lives by the opinion of others. Being authentic is the ability to make self-honoring choices and

stand firmly in who we are in our core. Being true to ourselves gives us the insight and compassion to see others for who they are, not who we expect them to be. It frees us up from the judgment of ourselves and others and it gives others the freedom to be themselves as well." [1]

~**Victoria J. Reynolds**

1   http://www.authentic-self.com/authentic-self-quotes.html

<u>Chapter 15</u>

Epilogue

"You were born an original. Don't die a copy." [1]

~ John Mason

---

1   http://www.quotegarden.com/be-self.html

Epilogue

In summary, a courageously authentic life in my opinion is the ONLY life worth living. It is the life you were DESTINED TO LIVE, the one you dreamed of as a child. This path will be a revelation to you and all those around you.

Hopefully this work has given you the courage and curiosity to rediscover **who you really are**, to tune in to what you are all about, what you want and to go for it. I mean REALLY go for it as if your life depended on it...because it does!

THIS IS NOT A PRACTICE LIFE! You don't get a redo, so act like it!

More importantly, I hope it has given you the courage to share 100% of yourself. Dare to share an absolutely amazing and unique person with the world. Remember, the world will be a MUCH better place for others once you live and share your total truth, no matter how inconvenient it may seem at times. Believe it or not, the world and this life CAN handle ALL of you all the time; you don't have to hold back anymore. Let go.

I want you to know that I respect you for having the courage to embark on this courageously authentic odyssey. Your life will thank you.

This is not a practice life! Go to it! You are so unique and beautiful, don't you dare ever forget that!

Onward and upward! I can't wait to hear of your journey living and loving your life in courageous authenticity. Send me an email at info@2BFRANK.ca. And/or participate in our discussions at Liveitbook.com.

Namaste!

Frank C. Maloney, MBA, BComm., CPCC

"Be brave enough to live life creatively. The creative is the place where no one else has ever been. You have to leave the city of your comfort and go into the wilderness of your intuition. You can't get there by bus, only by hard work and risk and by not quite knowing what you are doing. What you'll discover will be wonderful. What you'll discover will be yourself." [1]

~ Alan Alda

---

1 http://www.joyofquotes.com/courage_quotes.html

Appendix 1: Wheel of Life

The Wheel of Life Form

Directions

The eight sections in the Wheel of Life represent different aspects of your life. Seeing the center of the wheel as "0" and the outer edges as "10", rank your level of satisfaction with each life area by drawing a straight or curved line to create a new outer edge.

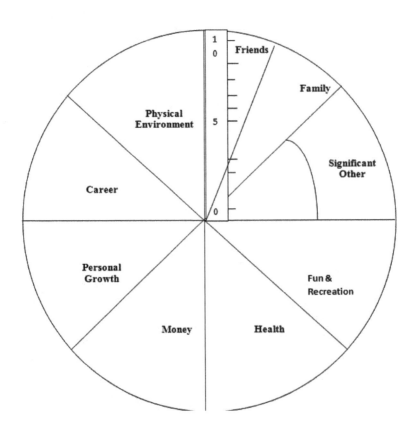

Appendix 2: The Abraham Hicks Emotional Scale

1. Appreciation/Empowerment/Freedom/Love
2. Passion
3. Enthusiasm/Eagerness/Happiness
4. Positive Expectation/Belief (Faith, added by FM)
5. Optimism
6. Hopefulness
7. Contentment
8. Boredom
9. Pessimism
10. Frustration/Irritation/Impatience
11. Overwhelment (completely overwhelmed, added by FM)
12. Disappointment
13. Doubt
14. Worry
15. Blame
16. Discouragement
17. Anger
18. Revenge
19. Hatred/Rage
20. Jealousy
21. Insecurity/Guilt/Unworthiness
22. Fear/Grief/Depression/Despair/Powerlessness

Appendix 3: My Live It! Experience (Over 1 Year)

Although difficult to summarize my Live It! experience in one page, it's worth a try!

1. Created a 10 foot wide, 5 foot tall vision wall of all I wanted in my life.

2. Wrote three self-help books, self-published one ("Cobra in the Closet").

3. Wrote seven episodes of an illustrated children's story.

4. Re-launched my coaching practice.

5. After years of dreaming of doing so, I took charge and began inspirational speaking.

6. Successfully transitioned out of a toxic intimate relationship.

7. Focused on having more close male friends and now have many.

8. Created and launched a weekly LoA newsletter and call-in radio show.

9. Experimented and created a psycho-social personal connection game (Masks-Off!).

10. Attracted a highly intuitive, passionate and connected relationship.

11. Re-created and strengthened difficult family relationships.

12. Began saying NO more regularly with much less guilt/worry. Began truly respecting my unique self, qualities and needs.

13. Realized that my "please other people" outlook was not what I wanted and began clearly and deliberately asking for and getting my needs met in an honest, non-manipulative way.

14. Began training my mind to do whatever I wanted, realizing my Inner World of thoughts shapes the Outer World of circumstances and events.

15. Really began living powerfully in the moment being my most brilliant self as often as I could and continue to.

16. Learned to look for beauty in the world and people.

17. Began practicing appreciation for little and many things very often.

18. Began the impossible (in a fun way) mission of leaving all people I meet better than when I met them.

19. Began courageously and clearly asking people for what I want and became committed to asking.

20. Realized and began applying that "all outside of me was not under my control" and started focusing rabidly on all I COULD control.

21. Began choosing joy, empowerment, love, appreciation, freedom and passion as my consistent objective.

22. Began embracing an "abundance" rather than "scarcity" view of the world, allowing abundance into my life.

23. Began learning to focus on WHAT I wanted and the critical WHY I wanted it, letting go of WHEN and HOW it would all happen.

24. I learned and live the distinction of being "committed" to doing my best but not "attached" to any particular outcome.

Appendix 4: Masculine and Feminine Diagram

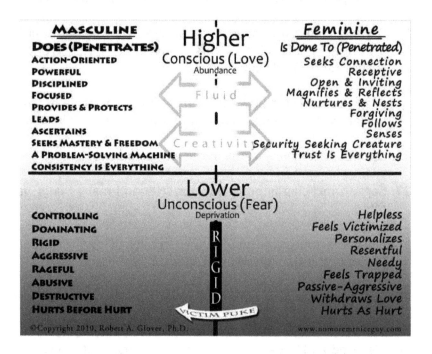

About the Author

Originally from Montreal, Quebec, Frank has been in Toronto since 1999. He obtained his Bachelor of Commerce at McGill University and his MBA in Strategy at Colorado's ISIM.

Frank is a Tony Robbins trained and a Coaches Training Institute certified Breakthrough Coach/ Mentor. He is the founder of 2BFRANK, www.2BFRANK.ca. He is an inspirational pioneer, blending the Law of Attraction and mind power in his coaching, inspirational speaking, men's and blended circles, and writing. He is a man who touches all who meet him deeply and permanently. His passion and joy is for a life inspired by choice, integrity and courageous authenticity.

He currently has three books to his credit, *"Killing Yourself With Your Fork?!"* on healthy living, *"The Career Chameleon"* on career transition and *"Cobra in the Closet: Roadmap to Realization"* about difficult relationships and how to thrive regardless of our external circumstances.